Effortless Change

by
Andrew Wommack

Harrison House
Tulsa, OK

21 20 19 18   11 10

EffortlessChange
ISBN 10: 160683-186-0
ISBN 13: 978-160683-186-1

Copyright © 2010 by Andrew Wommack Ministries, Inc.
850 Elkton Dr.
Colorado Springs, CO 80907

Published by Harrison House Publishers
Tulsa, Oklahoma 74145
www.harrisonhouse.com

Contents

Foreword

This book is going to inspire you as it inspired us. Andrew Wommack has the ability to break down Bible truths so we can understand and digest them in our hearts and allow them to transform our lives.

Do you need a change? Do you long to have God's power at work in you?

Change is possible if you just make the effort to hold God's perspective—God's Word—as truth in you. Just as a seed planted in soil naturally springs up with growth, the Word of God manifests itself in your life without your effort if you allow it to take up space in your heart.

The musical *God with Us* tells the story of the first church in Rome. The early believers were under pressure as persecution of the Christian faith increased. In these circumstances, the apostle Peter strengthened the followers of Jesus in their faith in the midst of hardship.

By sharing God's Word and from his own walk with Jesus, Peter turned their attention from their fears to God's promises by reminding them what God had done. Trusting God is always the answer! Even when faced with the threat of death, assurance in the new life and the resurrection of Jesus empowered early believers to overcome.

By believing in God's Word—making His perspective truth in your life and situation—it will *effortlessly* change you.

Elizabeth Muren
Artistic Director of Holy Land Experience

Introduction

Effortless change—it sounds impossible. Yet, that's what the Word reveals about how the kingdom of God works.

Most people view change as a difficult, painful, and labor-intensive process. To their way of thinking, it takes a huge amount of effort to change their thoughts, actions, and circumstances. Due to this, change is something they resist. It's hard to change routines, traditions, and long-standing problems. People get stuck in ruts—ways of thinking and doing - therefore, there's just a natural resistance toward change.

In this book, I want to share with you some truths from the Word of God that can totally transform the way you understand and approach change. If you receive these truths into your heart and apply them to your life, you'll be able to see change take place in your life effortlessly.

While many people don't recognize their need to change, others are very aware, and have a strong desire to change. If you're sick, you probably desire to walk in health. If you're in poverty, it's likely that you want to experience more of God's financial provision. You may realize that you would like certain changes in your life externally. However, all true change begins internally. It starts with what's on the inside of you.

Taking the Limits Off God

On January 31, 2002, the Lord spoke to me in a personal and powerful way. He told me that I had been limiting what He wanted to do in and through my life because of my small thinking. This word literally shook my world, so I spent about a week or so really meditating on this until it became a revelation in my life. Then I called my staff together and told them what God had convicted me of, saying, "I don't know how long it will take to change the image that's inside me. It may take a week, a month, a year, five years—I don't know. But I am going to change, and we will start seeing increase!" I remember that within one week, things started happening so quickly that it just amazed me.

Before I even had time to write a letter, send it to our mailing list, and receive a response (which normally takes at least three months), we saw a huge financial increase. All that had changed was inside me—my attitude, thoughts, and expectations. Other than that, we weren't doing anything differently. Yet, we immediately set records three months in a row in receipts from people. This was before my letter on this subject went out—before the people had a chance to even hear what God had said to me and respond! When I changed on the *inside*, immediately everything in my life began to change on the *outside*. This example is just one of many I have personally experienced. External change began to manifest on the outside when I started to change the way I thought on the inside.

If you want to see change outwardly, it has to begin on the inside. That's what this book is all about—how to start changing on the inside. If you can change the way you think—the way you are on the inside—then you'll see a change on the outside...effortlessly.

Chapter 1

It Begins on the Inside

The Word of God clearly reveals that as you think in your heart, so are you.

For as he thinketh in his heart, so is he.

Proverbs 23:7

If you can't—or should I say won't—change on the inside, then you aren't going to see change on the outside. You can pray, beg God, and get other people to intercede for you all you want. They could even lay hands on you until they rub all the hair off the top of your head, but you aren't going to see change in your life externally until you change internally.

Many people say, "But I do desire to change. I've done everything I know, yet it seems like things are just continually the same." God's Word is true. As you think in your heart, so are you. (Proverbs 23:7.) This is a law of God. Romans 8:6 confirms this truth, revealing that:

To be carnally minded is death; but to be spiritually minded is life and peace.

Before you take offense at my words, resenting and disagreeing with what I'm sharing, consider this truth. Of course, everyone has a bump in the road now and again, whether they are walking with the Lord or not. We live in a fallen world, and we have an enemy that comes against us. Not every single problem is a direct result of something flawed on the inside of us. However, if your overall life is spiraling downward, if nothing ever works and problems are all you seem to experience, then you should stop and consider that perhaps your inner man may need some work.

What Have You Planted?

People typically respond to tough circumstances and situations by blaming someone or something else. "It's the color of my skin. It's my family background. I was disadvantaged." They'll blame anybody. "This person mistreated me. It's my employer who's the jerk, not me." It's always somebody else's fault.

However, the Word makes it clear that your experience, your surroundings—everything about you—is basically a result of the way you think. As you think in your heart, that's the way it is. When you think spiritually minded thoughts, you get life and peace. When you don't, you get death. (Romans 8:6.) You may not like that. You might be saying, "No, that's not true," but it is.

If I came over to your house to see your garden, I wouldn't have had to be with you in the beginning when you sowed the seeds to know what you've planted. All I'd have to do is observe the plants that are growing up. If you have corn growing there, you planted corn. If there are peas, you sowed peas. You may claim that someone else came in and planted something in your garden you did not intend. However ultimately, it's your responsibility to guard and protect your garden. Whatever is growing there is what you've planted or what you've allowed to be planted there.

It Begins on the Inside

Just as this is true in the natural realm, it's true in the spiritual realm. Whatever is growing in the garden of your life is what you've planted or allowed to be planted in your heart. Before you can really see change, you must quit using excuses and blaming anybody and everybody else for what is wrong in your life. You have to stop saying, "It's just fate," or "bad luck," or "nothing ever works for me." Scripture reveals that as you think in your heart, that's the way you're going to be. (Proverbs 23:7.) If you think spiritually minded, your thoughts will produce life and peace. (Romans 8:6.)

The Knowledge of God

Second Peter 1:2 further substantiates the principle that your thought life produces a harvest in the natural realm, when it says:

Grace and peace be multiplied unto you through the knowledge of God, and of Jesus our Lord.

Many people want grace and peace to be multiplied to them. They desire peace in their life, and they're praying for it. They may even be asking other people to help them get it. Actually, they're looking for peace to come externally—from outside them—into their circumstances. These words in 2 Peter 1:2 reveal that peace comes through the knowledge of God.

Peace in your life isn't the absence of problems or challenging circumstances around you. *God's kind of peace is there even in the midst of a storm.* It resides on the inside. Then, eventually, that peace on the inside of you will begin to change your circumstances on the outside.

Effortless Change

According as his divine power hath given unto us all things that pertain unto life and godliness, through the knowledge of him that hath called us to glory and virtue.

2 Peter 1:3

This verse says that God's divine power has (past tense) already given to us all things. Most people want God to just come with His power from the outside, in. They pray, "Oh Lord, stretch forth Your mighty hand and touch me!" They're looking for God to send a spiritual bolt of lightning to hit them and then—BOOM—they're healed, prospered, delivered, or whatever they need. However, this scripture says that all things that pertain to life and godliness come through the knowledge of God. This includes healing, prosperity, deliverance, joy, peace, success in business, good relationships, and anything else. Everything that pertains to life and godliness comes through the knowledge of God. This means that the born again Christian already has the peace of God in their spirit. As they renew their mind to who they are and what they have in Christ, they draw that peace out into their experience.

The dominant experience of your life is a reflection of the way you are thinking on the inside. (Proverbs 23:7.) Instead of looking for a change to take place externally in everybody and everything else around you, the first thing you need to do is recognize that change begins on the inside of you. This occurs according to the knowledge that you have of God. (2 Peter 1:2-3.)

Reality

This is a simple truth we are discovering, but it's profound. In fact, most people miss it because it's so simple, thinking, *No, it must be more complex than that. My present reality can't just be the result of not thinking properly about things*. God's Word is true. You can turn any circumstance in your life around by getting God's perspective and starting to think His thoughts. Some people call this by different names, but I believe this is what the Bible calls faith.

Faith is simply seeing things from God's perspective. When someone does something to you, instead of just reacting in the natural, physical realm, based on your emotions, faith considers, "What does God's Word say?" So you take a scripture like Ephesians 6:12, which says that you aren't wrestling...

> ...*against flesh and blood, but against principalities, against powers, against the rulers of the darkness of this world, against spiritual wickedness in high places.*

Instead of just focusing on the fact that a person has pushed your hot button, because of God's knowledge that you have through His Word, you recognize that the devil can speak through people and use them to come against you. Instead of just seeing things in the natural, you have a different perspective because of the knowledge of God. You think differently on the inside. You realize that your struggle is not really with that person who is angry at you, but with the one who is resisting God who is inside you. Because of this, you are able to respond differently to these situations than other people do. You turn around and love those people who are against you instead of getting into strife, and it produces different results. All of this begins with you thinking differently.

I could give you hundreds of testimonies from my life and the lives of others who have personally experienced this truth. This is reality. The world is full of people who want change in their circumstances, but few recognize that the change begins on the inside of them.

Insanity

At each of our Gospel Truth Seminars, I tell people about our Bible colleges. During my remarks, I often ask, "How many of you realize that there's more? How many of you desire more and want change in your life?" It's not unusual to see eighty to ninety percent of the crowd respond. Most of these are Christians—Spirit-filled believers—who recognize that there needs to be change in their lives. They aren't satisfied with where they are and they want something more.

After all these people admit, "Yes, I want change," I come back and ask, "What are you going to do to effect change? What is going to be any different?" One of the definitions of insanity is to do the same thing over and over again, and expect different results. If you want something to change on the outside, then you're going to have to start by changing something on the inside. You cannot keep the same internal thought processes and believe that your external circumstances will change. That, by definition, is insane! First of all, you must change in your heart. Then you'll have to take some steps to cooperate with that change. Change isn't going to come from the outside. It begins on the inside. If you want change in your life, then you're going to have to do something differently in your spirit.

The moment I bring this up this truth, I instantly meet resistance because people are afraid to change. I've actually met people before who were in terrible, miserable situations, yet they had adjusted to them. They knew they could survive. It may not have been what they wanted—their dream or goal—but they had been in their situation a long time. They knew that they could survive, and they were afraid of failure should they try to change their reality.

If that's you, one of the things that must happen in order to effect change in your life is you're going to have to get to a place where you are sick and tired of being sick and tired. You have to really reach a place where you say, "I'm going to do whatever it takes to see these changes externally happen in my life. I'm going to start changing the way I think. I'm going to start taking some risks." Unless you're willing to do these things, you'll never see this external change.

"How Long?"

The Bible relates the story of when the city of Samaria was surrounded and besieged by the Assyrian army. (See 2 Kings 6:24-7:20.) The Samaritans were starving to the extent that they were eating their own children. Animal dung, being sold as food, was commanding a high price. This city was suffering terribly from the siege, drought, and famine. The people were just about to be completely destroyed, yet they couldn't do anything about it because the Syrians had Samaria completely surrounded.

Four lepers sat at the gate of Samaria. As they talked to each other, they said, "How long are we going to sit here—until we die? If we stay here, we'll die. If we go into the city, the famine will destroy us. Let's go out to the Syrians. If they kill us, we're just going to die here anyway. We don't have anything to lose. Perhaps they'll show us mercy." (See 2 Kings 7:3-4.)

So these four lepers got up and went into the Syrian camp. It turned out that the Lord had already been there. He had caused the Syrians to hear a noise. They thought the Israelites had hired another nation to fight against them, so they had fled in terror, leaving behind all their food, animals, tents, provisions, gold, and silver. The Syrians had fled for their lives and left everything behind!

These four lepers, who were facing starvation just a few minutes before, experienced a tremendous personal deliverance. They went out to the camp and discovered food that was still warm. They began to eat their fill. They found clothes, gold, and silver. After finding all these things, eventually they were the ones who brought the good news back to the city of Samaria. They became the heroes who actually proclaimed deliverance to the entire area. All this happened because four lepers, shunned by their city, sitting out at the gates, starving to death, finally made a decision. Even though their outlook seemed terrible, they declared, "We've got to do something. We're going to die if we stay where we are. We must head in some direction." So they considered their options. Even though this option to go to the enemy camp didn't look real good, it was better than sitting still and dying. And because they did something different, they experienced tremendous deliverance.

Change Is Needed

Right now you may be dying like the four lepers. If not physically, then perhaps emotionally. You know you're dying. Your marriage is falling apart. Things aren't going right. You're keenly aware that something is wrong. You know there's more, yet you are fearful to take any steps because you're afraid you might fail. If you would just look at things properly, you'd realize that you're failing now. Even if you have a guaranteed income, live in a relatively nice house, and your circumstances are going well, if you aren't satisfied and fulfilled in your heart, then you are dying on the inside and change is necessary. If you don't wake up in the morning and feel like, "Praise God, another opportunity to do what the Lord has called me to do and make a difference in this world," then whether you realize it or not, change is needed.

If you want different results, then you're going to have to do something differently. To keep doing the same thing over and over again, while praying for different results, is insane. If you want different results, do something differently.

True change begins on the inside. You can sit there and pray for God to just supernaturally do something. Many people are praying to win the lottery, or have their circumstances change on some other roll of the dice. If that's what you are believing for, you aren't following God. That's not the way He's going to meet your need. The odds of that happening are millions to one. Nobody is going to walk into your office and out of the blue ask you to become the CEO of a Fortune 500 company. That's not how life works. Change doesn't happen that way. If you want change on the outside, it begins on the inside.

Effortless Change

Chapter 2

Meditate on the Word

I remember when the Word of God first came alive to me. It was immediately after my life-changing encounter with the Lord on March 23, 1968. The Bible was no longer just a book about what God said. As I read it, I knew the Lord was speaking directly to me. I just fell in love with the Word. When I studied it, the Lord imparted truths to me. I could tell that change was happening in my life.

I remember one instance when the Lord spoke to me and gave me a vision of what He wanted to do through me. He had already impacted my life, and I felt called to the ministry. I was in my bedroom at home, and still single at the time. I saw in my heart some of the things that God wanted to do in my life. While kneeling down beside my bed and praying with my Bible open in front of me, I was just overwhelmed when I thought about seeing blind eyes opened, deaf ears hearing, people raised from the dead—all kinds of miracles. I knew that God had called me to teach His Word and that people's lives would be changed. As an eighteen-year-old young man, I was praying over all these things.

Then I remember having a kind of a vision of many different things happening, including me ministering to people on television, just like I do now. I saw these things, and knew they were going to happen. Yet, I was an introvert. I couldn't even look a person in the face and talk to them. How was an introverted hick from Texas ever going to be on radio or television? I surely wouldn't have chosen me for that responsibility.

"How Do I Do This?"

So there I was, seeing in my heart a vision of all these things that God was calling me to do—seeing the absolute impossibility of it all in the natural realm. I was kneeling by my bed, praying, and asking, "Lord, how do I get from where I am to where I know You're telling me I'm supposed to go? It seems like such a huge distance, and I don't have a track to run on. I don't know how to get there. How do I do this?"

As I was praying, I just opened my eyes and looked. There was my Bible laying open on the bed in front of me. When I saw it, I heard the Lord say, "If you will take My Word and meditate on it day and night, then My Word will teach you everything you need to know. My Word will change everything."

I know that sounds really simple, but if it hadn't been so simple, I wouldn't have been able to get it! I took that word as God's direction to me. From that time forward, I just poured myself into the Word of God. I didn't think about all of the things that needed to happen for that vision to come to pass. I didn't keep asking, "Lord, how do I overcome my shyness? How do I get the money? How do I overcome this and do that?" I just forgot all of those issues, and immersed myself for long periods of time in God's Word. Up until the time I got married, I was spending anywhere from ten to sixteen hours a day studying the Word and learning the truths of

God. As I took God's Word and meditated on it day and night, it began to change me.

God is no respecter of persons. If you put His Word first place in your life and meditate on it on a consistent basis, it will change you.

Joshua

That's what God told Joshua to do. He was about to take over the leadership role from Moses. Now, if you stop and think about it, Moses would be a hard act to follow. Joshua must have been struggling with this new assignment, and asking, "God, what do I do? How do I lead these people?"

The Lord said to Joshua, "The same way I was with Moses, I will be with you. Wherever your feet trod, I'll give that land to you." (See Joshua 1:3,5.) God gave Joshua several promises, which are recorded in Joshua 1:1-7. Then He continued, saying:

This book of the law shall not depart out of thy mouth.

Joshua 1:8

Now, at this time all the people had were the first five books of the Bible, the ones that Moses had written out. Today because we have the completed scriptures, I believe that instead of "this book of the law," we can say, the Bible, the Word of God...

...shall not depart out of thy mouth; but thou shalt meditate therein day and night, that thou mayest observe to do according to all that is written therein: for then thou shalt make thy way prosperous, and then thou shalt have good success.

Joshua 1:8

13

Let's start at the end of this verse and work back. Most people want to be prosperous and have good success. Yet, I find it amazing that the vast majority of people bypass the first part of this verse. They'll spend their prayer time asking God to "please prosper my business, please cause my marriage to succeed, please heal my body," but they won't do what the Word says. Joshua 1:8 reveals that the way you get prosperity and good success in every area of your life is to take the Word of God and meditate on it to the degree that it saturates what you think about, what you talk about, and how you act. When God's Word literally begins to control your life, you will prosper and have good success physically, emotionally, relationally, financially—in every area.

I'm living proof of this truth. This is exactly what my life is based upon.

Focusing Your Attention

You may be thinking, *But Andrew, I work a job. I can't meditate on the Word day and night.* Or you may be saying, "I have two or three kids at home. I'm constantly running around here and there, doing this and that. I can't just sit there reading my Bible, and not pay any attention to what's going on with my children." Most people don't believe that you can literally meditate on the Word of God day and night. They think that this is a totally impractical demand. They don't understand the true definition of meditation. Meditation is simply focusing your attention on something to the point that it never leaves your consciousness.

Worry is meditation. It's just meditation on something negative or evil. Whatever your daily demands are—watching children, running errands, cleaning the house, taking your kids places, preparing food—you've gone through days accomplishing all of these activities, while at the same time your mind was fixed on thinking, *How am I going to pay for this? What are we going to do? Is my spouse running around on me? Are they with someone? Are we heading for a divorce?* You were able to do all the things you needed to do, yet your mind still worried about those other things.

In your career, you could be doing whatever kind of job you do, yet in your mind you may still be thinking, *How is this situation going to work out?* You could be sitting there working, yet have something else occupying your mind. You're worrying about this issue day and night. If you're honest, there have probably been times when certain problems have bothered you to the point where you dream about them. You experience a fitful night of sleep because your mind was still stayed on, *What am I going to do? How am I going to get out of this situation?* That's worry, which is a form of meditation.

The part of you that worries is the exact same part of you that meditates. Meditation is just focused on positive things.

If you have children at home or you're working a job, it's wrong for you to sit down and study the Word sixteen hours a day. This is not being faithful to your family, boss, or employer—to the responsibilities you have been assigned. But you can take a passage of scripture, read it, and then meditate on it the rest of the day and night while attending to your responsibilities. You can be thinking on the Word of God and considering, *How does this apply to me?* while you're going about your daily activities.

"Believe!"

Last week I was studying the account of King Jehoshaphat found in 2 Chronicles 20. King Jehoshaphat had been faithful to the Lord and had served Him, yet three nations came out against him. The armies of these three nations joined together into what seemed, to King Jehoshaphat, to be an overwhelming force. There seemed to be no way for him and his people to win. So Jehoshaphat built a platform, assembled all of the people together, and addressed them. He stood up on the platform, lifted his hands to heaven in front of all the people, and began to pray. He said, "God, we don't have any help, any power, against this great multitude that has come against us. Our only help is in You. We're standing here. We're waiting on You. God, we need You to do something!" (See 2 Chronicles 20:12.)

At the conclusion of King Jehoshaphat's prayer, a prophet stood up and prophesied, "You won't even have to fight in this battle. In the morning, assemble yourself. You will go out and find that it has already been won." (See 2 Chronicles 2:17.) After this declaration from the prophet…

> …*Jehoshaphat stood and said, Hear me, O Judah, and ye inhabitants of Jerusalem; Believe in the LORD your God, so shall ye be established; believe his prophets, so shall ye prosper.*
> *2 Chronicles 20:20*

Jehoshaphat spoke powerful words of faith, saying, "Believe the word of God!" They arose very early the next morning and went out to meet these three armies that were coming against them. They didn't just say that they believed God; they proved it by acting on their faith and putting the singers up front. (See 2 Chronicles 2:21.)

As I've been meditating on this passage of scripture, I've thought, *What a miracle!* Some people read Bible stories like they didn't really happen, or maybe they do believe that these events actually took place, but they happened so long ago to somebody else so far away that they just don't connect. Don't just read the information in God's Word, begin to think about it. Consider, what if you were in the position of Jehoshaphat? What would it have been like to tell the soldiers to get in the back and to put the choir in the front? How must it have sounded as they sang, "Praise the Lord for His mercy endures forever" on their way out to meet the three armies (2 Chronicles 20:21)—over a million people armed to the hilt? These thoughts are the beginning of meditation.

It's one thing to read passage, but it's another thing to go deeper and meditate on it. I read those passages of scripture again and again for two or three days. I'd go back to the same passages and spend thirty minutes to an hour reading, looking up cross references, and gathering information. Then I'd spend time meditating on what I had read during the day. I was on an airplane traveling to a Gospel Truth Seminar. My eyes were closed, but I was thinking about what a huge step of faith this was for Jehoshaphat, and how God rewarded him.

All You Need

Sure enough, when the people of Judah came over the hill and looked, these three armies that had aligned against them had turned on each other. Two of them had agreed to kill the third. Then, after they wiped out that army, they began killing each other. The very last two people standing killed each other. So when the armies of Judah came over the hill, they looked and there was nothing but corpses. They found so much gold, silver, and clothes that it took the entire nation of Judah three days to gather the spoil.

Most people read through a Bible story like that and glibly say, "Oh, there was a victory for trusting God," but you can milk this passage for tremendous truths. Here was Jehoshaphat, his life and kingdom looked like they were just about to be snuffed out. In the midst of that, he cried out to God. The Lord gave him a prophecy. He believed it, and less than twenty-four hours after he began trusting God, the very thing that looked like it would be the destruction of the nation turned out to be one of the best things that ever happened. The people of Judah didn't even have to lift a sword. They went out and gathered much spoil, and Jehoshaphat dedicated all of it to the temple. Prior to that time, some other people had come in and stolen all of the gold and silver out of the temple. Through faith in the word God had given him, Jehoshaphat saw this situation that looked like it was going to be his destruction turn out to be the very thing God used to supply the needed resources to refurbish the temple. It turned out great!

For days after I read this passage, I just meditated on those scriptures, thinking about how those truths applied to my life and some of the problems that faced me that made it appear like it could be the end of Andrew Wommack Ministries. Rather than worry about my circumstances, I began thinking that in the same way that God acted on behalf of Jehoshaphat, He could do it for me. The situation that looked like it could destroy me, could very well turn out to be one of the best things that ever happened to me.

Meditate on the Word

As you meditate on the Word, faith rises. Many people miss this increase in faith because they read the Word, but don't meditate on it. Everyone reading this may not be able to spend large quantities of time in the Word but everyone can meditate on it day and night.

Regardless of what your circumstances or problems are, you're never more than one word from God away from absolute victory. The Lord knows exactly where you are and how to get you to where you're supposed to be. All you need is just the slightest instruction, an impartation of God's wisdom. All you need is a word from God!

Effortless Change

Chapter 3

God Speaking

God isn't wringing His hands and wondering how He can pull a situation out for you. There is a simple solution for every person. Our biggest problem is our inability to hear God's voice. The way we know what God is saying is through His Word. If we would get into the Word of God and meditate on it, the Lord would speak to us. He could give us wisdom and direction.

I deal with all kinds of people all around the world. They vary greatly in maturity. Many of them nod their heads and tell me, "We know that this is God's Word, and it has our answers." They say that because they know it's what they're supposed to say, but in a practical sense, most people don't really believe that they can solve their problems at work, at home—anywhere—by the Word of God.

Wisdom and Instruction

In Proverbs, chapter 1, Solomon described why he wrote the book that would follow:

To know wisdom and instruction; to perceive the words of understanding; To receive the instruction of wisdom, justice, and judgment, and equity; To give subtilty to the simple, to the young man knowledge and discretion.

Proverbs 1:2-4

Solomon said the book of Proverbs was meant to give wisdom to the simple and understanding to those who don't have any. Then he spoke about the good this wisdom and understanding will bring you and the bad it will help you avoid. The truths contained in the book of Proverbs alone will instruct you concerning all kinds of things.

> *A man's gift maketh room for him, and bringeth him before great men.*
>
> Proverbs 18:16

This verse isn't talking about just your talents and abilities. Literally, it's speaking of a gift—a present given to a person. The negative side of this truth is a bribe. It's easy to understand how a bribe can affect people and change things. Yet gifts have tremendous potential for positive influence as well.

Another proverb says:

> *Cast out the scorner, and contention shall go out; yea, strife and reproach shall cease.*
>
> Proverbs 22:10

I've applied this in my own ministry. When there are problems among people, go to the person who is the root of it. Cast out the scorner—the critical person who's stirring everything up—and contention, strife, and reproach will cease.

Perfect Representation

Through God's Word, you can learn how to deal with people. You can gain wisdom if you're a boss, an employee, or a salesperson.

If you are a parent and you're struggling with your children, there's a wealth of information in the Bible. I have yet to run across a problem in life for which the Word of God doesn't provide an answer. And if you will take this Word, meditate on it, and put this knowledge on the inside of you, then the Holy Spirit will, at the appropriate time, quicken things to you and show you what to do.

God speaks to me this way. This is what makes my life tick. What has changed my life is my love for the Word of God.

I have sometimes faced criticism from people who say, "You love the Word of God more than you love God." I don't separate the two! Jesus is the Word made flesh who dwelt among us. (John 1:14.) When I refer to the Word, I'm not talking about just a physical book. You could tear a page out of the Bible, even a whole book, but you haven't changed the Word of God. The words contained in the Bible perfectly represent the heart of God.

When I read the Word, I'm not reading a book about God. This is the Lord writing to me! Even some of these things that were said thousands of years ago to other people, He speaks to me afresh today.

"I'll Give You Anything"

The Lord told Jeremiah:

Before I formed thee in the belly I knew thee; and before thou camest forth out of the womb I sanctified thee, and I ordained thee a prophet unto the nations.

Jeremiah 1:5

23

Some people read that and say, "Well, this was something written specifically to Jeremiah over three thousand years ago. Yet, here you are getting excited over it as if it was written to you!"

I can tell you the exact time and place where God spoke that word to me. I was in an apartment in Kingsley Place apartments in Dallas, Texas, in 1973. I read those scriptures and went to bed, but couldn't fall asleep (which was very unusual for me). I wondered, *What is going on?* Then all of a sudden, the presence of God manifested in that room. This took place soon after Jamie and I were married. I got up and went into our living room. The Lord came to me and said, just as He had with Solomon, "I'll give you anything you ask for." So I answered, saying, "I want the ability to speak Your Word effectively, so that it changes people's lives." Then He touched me, and led me to Jeremiah 1:5, saying:

> *Before I formed thee in the belly I knew thee; and before thou camest forth out of the womb I sanctified thee, and I ordained thee a prophet unto the nations.*

Then He continued speaking to me, saying:

> *Behold, I will make my words in thy mouth fire, and this people wood, and it shall devour them.*
>
> *Jeremiah 5:14*

Yes, God did speak these words to Jeremiah thousands of years ago, but He has also spoken them to me. They're mine. Say what you will, but the truth of this experience is working for me. I'm seeing the power of God manifest. This is an important way God has spoken to me in my life—through His Word.

Alive, Not Dead

Some folks say, "Well, I want God just to speak to me outside of His Word." I don't need that. I really believe that God inspired people to write down His Word. Many others have given their lives to preserve it. Many people take God's Word for granted. They don't respect and honor it for what it is—God speaking to us. That's why they don't get the benefit out of it that I do. Believe me, God's Word has everything in it that you need to succeed. If we would simply do what the Word says, and meditate on it day and night, we would prosper and have good success. (Joshua 1:8.)

The average person doesn't believe the truth that God's Word contains everything necessary for success. That's why they don't meditate on the Word of God day and night, which is the reason they're not prospering and succeeding more than they are.

Many Christians don't honor the Word of God by looking at it as literally God speaking to them. When they read it, they do it more out of religious obligation and duty. They don't read the Word expecting God to speak to them.

When I open up the Word of God, I literally view it as God talking to me—and He does. These are living words. The Bible is alive, it's not dead. (Hebrews 4:12.) There's a difference between this Book and any other book. That's why I choose not to read very much else. I might read one or two other books in a year, and that's mainly because I have so many people pressing me to read their book. Usually these books have been written by people I like and know that they have some good things to say. However, my supreme desire is for the Word. Everything I need is right there in the Word of God.

A man came up to me recently at one of my meetings in California. He told me that he had really enjoyed the ministry, that the message blessed him, and that he hadn't heard the truths I had shared that day, before. Since he was a scientist, he told me, "You ought to read this and that book about science and the Bible. Then you could get to where you could come at the Bible from a scientific perspective and answer all of these questions, and so forth." He gave me several books, and really wanted me to read them.

The Real Thing

Finally, because this man kept pushing me so hard, I had to push back. I didn't do it out of anger or anything like that. I just told him, "The way people learn how to recognize counterfeit money isn't by studying all of the counterfeits. There are so many different ways to counterfeit money that you just can't learn every counterfeit. Instead, the people who are going to be on the front lines of deciding which bills are counterfeit or not are given the real thing. They study the grain, the weight, the texture, the look—everything about genuine bills. In the process, they become so familiar with the real that they're able to instantly recognize a counterfeit.

"That's how I feel about God and His Word. I'm just going to become so familiar with God through His Word that I don't have to go to this person over here or learn this, that, and these other things. I'm just going to become so single-minded, so focused on the Word of God, that I don't have to have all these supplemental things."

God Speaking

I realize that this is a departure from how most people live. Most people advocate reading a book a week, a book a month, or something like that. I'm not saying that's wrong or of the devil. I'm just saying that there is a definite difference between anybody else's book and the Word of God!

I've written books. In fact, you're reading one right now. So it's obvious I'm not against books. But there is a difference between my books and the Word of God. The only reason I like my books as much as I do is because they're crammed full of the Word of God. Actually, my purpose in writing books is simply to explain truths and share personal examples in order to help people understand the Word of God. However, it wouldn't bother me one bit if you bypassed all of my books and just meditated on the Word of God day and night. You'd be better off.

Take God's Word. Meditate on it day and night. Get to where the Word of God is more real to you than the person sitting next to you on the bus. When you're at work, even though you interact with people and do your job well, may the truth be that you're constantly thinking about scriptures and what God is speaking to you. Meditate on God's Word and try to relate it to different circumstances and situations. If you would do that, you would prosper more accidentally than you ever have on purpose.

Give Attention

Proverbs says:

My son, attend to my words; incline thine ear unto my sayings.

Proverbs 4:20

"Attend to my words" simply means give attention. You've been in school before when the teacher was up there talking, and even though you were looking straight at her, you weren't attending to her words. The words were going in one ear and out the other. You were daydreaming. Your focus was somewhere else.

Likewise, many people go through the motions of reading passages of scripture without truly attending to the words they are reading. You could probably read an entire chapter of the Word in no time, and then close your Bible as soon as you're done. But if I immediately came up to you and asked, "What chapter were you reading? What book of the Bible was it in?" you wouldn't even have a clue. You certainly couldn't tell me what you read. I'm not trying to condemn you, I just want you to realize how often you fail to attend to His words.

Life and Health

Whenever I emphasize how important and powerful God's Word is, people always come back to me and say, "I've studied the Bible. I've read the Word. In fact, I've read the Bible all the way through and it hasn't done what you describe for me." To have the Word be effective in your life, you must do what Proverbs 4 says, which is to attend to God's words and incline your ear.

The phrase "incline thine ear" isn't telling you to change the position of your head. It's talking about listening with your heart. It's speaking of focus and commitment. You must listen to God's Word with your heart, not just your head.

God Speaking

Place a high priority and value on the Word of God. Start taking each one of these words as being a direct word from God to you. Attend to it. Incline your ear to it. Then you'll start getting the results I'm describing.

> *My son, attend to my words; incline thine ear unto my sayings. Let them not depart from thine eyes; keep them in the midst of thine heart. For they [God's words] are life unto those that find them, and health to all their flesh.*
>
> *Proverbs 4:20-22*

God's Word is life. No matter how grave the situation you're in, God's Word is life and health to all your flesh!

Effortless Change

Chapter 4

Transformed

If you're struggling with depression, you're not meditating on the Word of God day and night. Romans 8:6 reveals:

For to be carnally minded is death; but to be spiritually minded is life and peace.

If you have death in any form working in you—including depression, discouragement, anger, unforgiveness, bitterness, etc.—it's because you've planted death. I don't say this to condemn you, but rather to enlighten you and show you where the source of your problem lies.

Remember my earlier example when I said that I don't have to be with you when you plant a garden to see what you've sown. All I have to do is be there when the crop grows up to know what you've planted. If you have death in your life—if you're depressed, discouraged, angry, or bitter—you haven't been meditating on the Word of God. Spiritual mindedness only produces life and peace.

Take a Gos-pill

Jesus said:

The words that I speak unto you, they are spirit, and they are life.

John 6:63

31

Since God's Word is spirit, to be spiritually minded is to be Word of God minded. If you are Word of God minded, this will produce life and peace.

> *Thou wilt keep him in perfect peace, whose mind is stayed on thee: because he trusteth in thee.*
>
> Isaiah 26:3

Some might say, "But I've done all of these things, and I still have terrible problems in my life." I would say that you may have read the Word of God or heard somebody else quote it, but you haven't attended to it. You haven't inclined your ear and kept His sayings in the midst of your heart. (Proverbs 4:20-22.) You've let your eyes depart and focus on other things. If you do what God's Word says, it will produce the results that the Word said it will produce. Proverbs 4:20-22 reveals that God's Word will be life to those who find its sayings, and health to all their flesh.

Literally thousands of people have come to me with sickness in their body and have asked, "Would you pray for me?" Yes, I'll pray for you. But what does the person who is doing the praying for everybody else do when they get sick? Do I run to somebody every time I have an illness begin to fight against me? No, I go to the Word of God. Just like if you have a pain, you take a pill. If I have a pain, I take a Gos-pill. I take the Word of God.

Health Flows Through

Whenever I have any physical symptoms of illness hitting me, I'll stand against them, rebuke them, and speak my faith. Normally, that will take care of everything. I've lived now over forty years in Divine health. I took a couple of asprin after having a tooth removed and I got so weak once after ministering 82 times in two weeks that I had a sinus infection for a couple of days, but that's it. I don't get sick. I don't believe in being sick. But I've had the symptoms of sickness hit me and they'll last for an hour or two. If, after rebuking the symptoms, I don't see instantaneous results, then I take up the Word of God. I start going over scriptures that I already know, like 1 Peter 2:24, which says that by His stripes, I was healed. It's not good enough just to quote these scriptures from memory. I go back and look them up again because of this principle. God's words are life to those that find them, and health to all their flesh (Proverbs 4:22). The Word of God is health to your flesh!

> *He sent his word, and healed them, and delivered them from their destructions.*
>
> Psalm 107:20

If I need healing in my body, I take the Word of God and meditate on it. I eat these words because they're life and health to my flesh. I may even quote these words, but I'll still go back to my Bible and study them. As I do, the Bible reveals that:

> *Faith cometh by hearing, and hearing by the word of God.*
>
> Romans 10:17

Notice that verse doesn't say, "Faith comes by having heard." No. It's in the present tense. We have to continually hear God's Word. When I meditate on those scriptures, I stir up the faith that I already have on the inside of me. (Romans 12:3.) As I start meditating on the scriptures, health flows through me.

I've only gone a few hours, maximum, over the past forty years with any symptom of sickness in my body. I've overcome broken bones, swelling, sprains, fevers, upset stomachs, and nausea. I actually have a doctor's report saying that I had an incurable disease. Yet within hours of that doctor's visit, I was totally healed. I've operated this way for decades, allowing God's Word to bring life and health to my body, and it works.

This is what the Word of God teaches about itself. Yet most people, even those who say, "God's Word is important," don't really live as though it is important. They don't meditate on the Word day and night. That's the reason they don't have good success and aren't prosperous.

Made Manifest

God used the first two verses of Romans 12 to totally transform my life. It was the first passage of scripture that ever came alive to me back in 1967. These verses impacted me so deeply that they literally changed the course of my life.

> *I beseech you therefore, brethren, by the mercies of God, that ye present your bodies a living sacrifice, holy, acceptable unto God, which is your reasonable service. And be not conformed to this world: but be ye transformed by the renewing of your mind, that ye may prove what is that good, and acceptable, and perfect, will of God.*
>
> *Romans 12:1-2*

That's what I was seeking in my life. I wanted to know God's will. So I looked up the word "prove," and it means to make manifest to the physical senses. That was exactly what I desired – I wanted God's plan to be made manifest physically in my life. I knew that God already had a plan for my life. I believed that. I just didn't know what it was. It wasn't manifest to my physical senses. I believed it was there—somewhere. I just wanted it to be manifest. So for months, I focused on this passage of scripture. I wanted the result promised at the end of verse two, that I would make manifest to my physical senses the good, acceptable, and perfect will of God. So I went back to verse one and the beginning of verse two to see what I had to do to get to my desired end.

Verse one radically transformed my life and gave me a totally brand-new direction. After meditating on it for three and a half months, I had this experience where God poured out His love in my life. This happened on March 23, 1968, and it literally changed the course of my life. I've never been the same since.

As important as that experience was, I would have lost the benefit of this encounter with God if I had not continued to grow in the knowledge of God's Word. You may be struggling to understand that, thinking, *Oh, if I could only really encounter God. If I had a vision or if the Lord were to appear to me, then my life would never be the same.* I've had some very miraculous encounters with God, but I'm telling you that you can't just live off of an experience or emotions. It's been over forty years since I encountered God this way. If all I was living from was an experience that happened to me over forty years ago, I would be dry, dead, and lifeless today.

That encounter got me jump started. It opened up my eyes and gave me a vision. It provided me with motivation. That encounter was good, and I praise God for it, but what really changed my life was Romans 12:2:

> *Be not conformed to this world: but be ye transformed by the renewing of your mind.*

This is what's happened to me: I've been transformed by the renewing of my mind. I had this supernatural experience, which got my attention, changed my desires, and started me moving in a different direction. However, it is the renewing of my mind through the Word of God that has completely, thoroughly, and totally transformed me. I attribute every bit of the power and victory that I've experienced to the Word of God becoming alive and speaking to me.

Melted

Romans 12:2 says:

Be not conformed to this world.

The Greek word translated "conformed" here literally means to pour into the mold. You aren't going to exit this life the same way that you came in. You came in a baby—innocent, naïve, without a firm direction or plan for your life. By the time you live twenty, forty, sixty, or more years, the pressures of this life are going to melt you. Every one of us will be melted. You'll change shape, form, and direction. However, the good news is, you get to choose what mold you fit into.

The pressures of this life tend to try to force everybody into the world's mold of pessimism. When you lose your dreams and goals, you harbor unforgiveness and become bitter. That's the mold the problems in this life are trying to force you into. But you don't have to go into that mold. You can choose to be transformed.

I first truly understood this concept on the day that I received my orders to be shipped out to Vietnam. Like most of my fellow soldiers, I was still a teenager. At nineteen years of age, I had already been through my infantry training. Every one of the men I had been training with, except one, received orders to go to Vietnam. Immediately, most of these young men broke down in fear and started crying.

As I write this today, we're at war in Iraq. Many brave men and women have given their lives for the cause of freedom. Each one has a story, beloved family and friends who miss them, and unfulfilled hopes and dreams. However, the sheer volume of American blood that flowed in Vietnam so far exceeds the 1,700 deaths over two or three years in Iraq, that the casualty count pales in comparison. Although the car bombs and other dangers in Iraq are bad enough, it's nothing compared to what was happening in Vietnam at that time I received my orders. There were mortars, bombs, booby traps, and people with guns coming at you. When you got shipped to Vietnam, you knew you were going to come into contact with the enemy. It wasn't just some of the people over there who were getting shot at. It was everyone. Due to this, people were just falling apart left and right like two-dollar suitcases when they received their orders.

After we received our orders, while all these young men were weeping all over the room, the chaplain came in and made this statement: "Going to Vietnam is a fire, and it will melt you. But you get to pick what mold you fit into. This doesn't have to be a negative experience that destroys you. It can be a positive experience." God used that chaplain's words to speak directly to me.

Renew Your Mind

You may not be a soldier in the midst of a war zone, but you will still have pressures come against you in this life that will melt you. However, you get to pick whether you'll be like the other people who become negative, bitter, and unforgiving. You choose whether you'll murmur and complain, or if you'll let these things drive you to the Lord and make you stronger and more stable in your commitment to God. How do you make that choice?

> *Be not conformed to this world: but be ye transformed by the renewing of your mind, that ye may prove what is that good, and acceptable, and perfect, will of God.*
>
> *Romans 12:2*

The Greek word rendered "transformed" here is *metamorphoo*. It's the word from which we derive our English word "metamorphosis." A little worm spins a cocoon, and then, after time, comes out a beautiful butterfly. If you want to be transformed from something creepy, crawly, and earthbound into something beautiful that can fly, you need to be metamorphosed. Do you want to change from being weak, inferior, and bound by all kinds of problems into someone who releases and experiences the abundant life of God from within? The Word of God reveals that the way to do this by the renewing of your mind. You must renew your mind to the Word of God.

You can't just turn your mind off and think of nothing. Sometimes when you ask someone what they are thinking, they'll answer, "Nothing." The truth is, they were thinking of something. You can't *not* think. Your mind is constantly going. Even when you're asleep, your subconscious mind will inspire dreams. Whether you're

38

awake or not, you can't turn your mind off and not think. All you can do is choose what you think on—the things of the Lord or the things of the world.

The things of the world may simply be physical, natural things. They don't have to be demonic, X-rated, R-rated, terrible, ungodly things. They can be decent things. They don't have to be bad. But if you are occupied with the things of this world, you'll never experience this transformation.

The Greatest Thing in the World

If you want your mind to be transformed, like a caterpillar into a butterfly, the way you do it is by putting your mind on God through His Word. If you desire to be poured into God's mold, you do it by the Word of God. There is no other system that God has in place.

Now, you can experience a touch from God. He loves us, and especially in times of crisis, we can cry out to Him and He'll touch us. Some people call this an epiphany. You could have an encounter with the Lord. God could speak to you, and it would touch your life. But I guarantee you that these emotional types of experiences only last a very short period of time. You will never be able to sustain a relationship with God, and certainly not be able to be transformed, if your experience remains on an emotional level only.

You have to renew your mind. If you want to be transformed long-term and see your life change, you must be transformed by the Word. You must renew your mind. Some folks say, "That seems restrictive to me." To me, it's awesome. I love this truth because it's so simple. All that is required for transformation is that you just meditate on the Word day and night. (Joshua 1:8.) Keep the Lord and His truths in your thoughts. Go over and over them, keeping your mind stayed on the Word of God—not "as the stomach turns" on television. If you'll keep your mind stayed on the Lord by meditating on His Word, then without effort—automatically—your life will begin to change.

Some people really struggle to believe that this is true. If that's you, don't knock it until you've tried it. I've tried it. I have spent thousands, tens of thousands, perhaps even hundreds of thousands of hours meditating on the Word of God. There's nothing that challenges and inspires me more than being in the Word of God and hearing Him speak to me. All of a sudden, I will recognize an application between the principles I see in the scriptures or a certain Bible character's life and my own. God makes a direct connection between His Word and my life. The greatest thing in the world to me is to see or experience God speaking to me through His Word.

A By-product, Not the Cause

Many Christians don't feel this same way about God's Word. They've read the Bible. They may not have found it boring, but it wasn't as stimulating to them as a novel. Personally, I think the subject matter in God's Word beats any novel, any plot you could ever come up with. The Bible is full of so many wonderful things. Yet, many Christians just read it as a book and don't meet with God to receive from Him like He wants them to. They can't honestly say that spending time with God through His Word is the most exciting thing they've ever done.

I can truthfully say that the greatest joy and excitement I think I have ever had in my life has come when I have been alone with God studying His Word. All of a sudden, I connect with God's heart. I know what He is saying to me through the scriptures. God gives me a direct revelation. I can truthfully say that's the greatest thing that's ever happened in my life. I've seen several people raised from the dead, including my own son. I've seen great miracles and healings manifest. I'm not saying that these events weren't wonderful and exciting. They were, but it's the Word of God and my relationship with Him through His Word that has caused all those things to happen. They've been a by-product, not the cause. Renewing my mind to God's Word is what has turned my life around.

If you want to be transformed, the way you do it is to take God's Word and meditate on it day and night. Dwell on it, and it will change you. Now that's exciting!

Effortless Change

Chapter 5

Converting the Soul

I vividly remember what was going on in my life when the Lord showed me the importance of His Word. I had just made a commitment to Him. As I sought the Lord, I felt like He told me to drop out of college. This was during the Vietnam War, so for me to follow God in this meant I would be immediately drafted and sent to Vietnam. Also, I would lose the social security income that I had been receiving since my father's death. I could keep this income only as long as I was still in school. So following the Lord cost me financially. It sent me to a war zone where I quite possibly could have been killed. Beyond that, every person in my life whom I had ever looked up to until then told me one way or another, "This isn't God." They told me that this was of the devil and that if I was going to be a preacher, then I needed to get a seminary education. Everyone was telling me what a dunce I was, and how my ministry wouldn't happen unless I followed the prescribed way of doing things. I wasn't trying to rebel against the advice of these well meaning people. I just wanted to be obedient to what I knew God was speaking to me in my heart.

When I ran across these scriptures in Romans 12, God showed me that if I would take His Word and meditate on it, His Word would accomplish everything I needed in my life. I can't tell you how much comfort and direction that gave me at that crucial crossroads of my life. So I poured myself into the Word of God, and here I am over forty years later fulfilling God's will for my life. It's the revelation of God's Word that has transformed my life and ministry, and the same can be true for you.

All 176 verses of Psalm 119—the longest chapter in the Bible—are about the importance of God's Word. Consider these excerpts from this marvelous chapter:

> *Wherewithal shall a young man cleanse his way? by taking heed thereto according to thy word.*
>
> *Psalm 119:9*

> *Thy word have I hid in mine heart, that I might not sin against thee.*
>
> *Psalm 119:11*

> *Great peace have they which love thy law: and nothing shall offend them.*
>
> *Psalm 119:165*

Restored

Psalm 19 also affirms the importance of God's Word and how it will change your life. The different phrases in this Psalm like "the law of the LORD," "statutes of the LORD," "commandments of the LORD," and "testimony of the LORD" all just refer to the Word of God.

> *The law of the LORD is perfect, converting the soul.*
>
> *Psalm 19:7*

Converting the Soul

In Hebrew, this word rendered "converting" here means to turn back. Many people have experienced tragedy in their life. Their soul has been bruised, battered, and damaged. The average person just continues to carry this pain. They don't seem able to break free. Therefore, most people have just embraced their pain as just the way that life is supposed to be.

One of the reasons they accept this is because that's the way the world—apart from access to God's supernatural power—looks at life. In the natural realm, without God, that's true. You are a product of your environment. If you were verbally, physically, or sexually abused, that's going to scar you. If you were beat down, condemned, and told you could do nothing and would amount to nothing; that could very well influence you for the rest of your life.

However, God doesn't intend to just give you the ability to cope. He can totally change you so that it's just like those things never even happened. Through His Word, He wants to convert your soul—turn you back to the condition you were in before the cares of life pushed in on you. (Psalm 19:7.)

If you were damaged by something or someone, you don't have to bear that for five, ten, twenty, or thirty years. You can get over it. The Word of God will convert your soul and turn it back to what God meant it to be.

Wisdom

Since Adam and Eve's fall, our existence and surroundings have been so negative and different than what God originally intended them to be. By the time an average child graduates from high school, they've seen tens of thousands of brutal murders on television. They've been exposed to sexual immorality and ungodliness that the Lord never intended for mankind to be burdened with. How do you overcome all that? The law of the Lord is perfect—it's not just good. It's not just better than anything else that's out there. It's perfect; and it will convert—restore—your soul to its original condition.

So many people carry around baggage—hurts and pains from years before—from all kinds of things like previous marriages, losses, disappointments, and broken relationships. They just never seem to recover. That's because they aren't taking the Word of God and properly using it in their life. Psalm 19:7 tells us that God's Word is perfect. It will convert your soul. It will restore you to your original God-intended condition.

Psalm 19:7 continues, saying:

The testimony of the LORD is sure, making wise the simple.

God's Word makes wise the stupid—people who don't think properly and make mistakes.

I've heard all kinds of stories from people who made stupid decisions and suffered from it. They committed adultery and then wound up with shame and disgrace. They lost their job, their church, and their friends. They ended up with physical problems, like AIDS. On and on the list of repercussions go from the stupid things that we have done. Every once in a while I just want to ask folks, "How dumb can you get and still breathe?" It's amazing what some people do.

You may be thinking, *I've done some of those same things. I just don't seem to be able to help it.* Right here in Psalm 19:7, God's Word promises to give wisdom to the simple. God's Word will make you wise even if you have been stupid in the past. You don't have to submit to the lie that says, "Well, my mind just isn't as bright as somebody else's." The Word of God will quicken your thinking and give you understanding.

Get Happy

So many people are just depressed and defeated. They can't seem to find any reason to rejoice. They're struggling, and they give this reason and that excuse saying, "This and that happened to me." Do you know what God's Word says about those who are depressed and defeated?

The statutes of the LORD are right, rejoicing the heart.
Psalm 19:8

If you aren't full of joy, peace, and rejoicing, the problem isn't your circumstances (1 Peter 1:8.) If you have ashes, mourning, and a spirit of heaviness instead of the oil of joy and the garment of praise, it's due to the fact that there's a vacuum on the inside seeking to be filled. (Isaiah 61:3.) You don't know the truth of God's Word. The statutes of the Lord are right, and they will rejoice your heart. If you're discouraged, take the Word of God. Start speaking the promises of God to yourself. You can get happy in a hurry!

Psalm 19:8 continues, saying:

The commandment of the LORD is pure, enlightening the eyes.

Is it worth the effort of meditating on God's Word to be able to see clearly instead of having a negative perception that always makes every cup look half empty? What a benefit it is to be able to see the positive side and to see a way through everything. That's what the Word of God does.

Great Reward

The fear of the LORD is clean, enduring for ever: the judgments of the LORD are true and righteous altogether. More to be desired are they than gold, yea, than much fine gold: sweeter also than honey and the honeycomb.

Psalm 19:9-10

God's Word is worth far more to me than gold, even much fine gold. To me, the Word of God is better than honey. How would you treat God's Word if you truly desired it more than money—even large amounts of it—and more than your favorite food? You'd be able to say along with Job:

I have esteemed the words of his mouth more than my necessary food.

Job 23:12

If you were to seek God through His Word like that, your life would be transformed.

Moreover by them is thy servant warned: and in keeping of them there is great reward.

Psalm 19:11

How much benefit would it be to your life if you could be warned before you get into a problem, pursue an ungodly relationship, take the wrong job, buy the wrong car, do something that damages your health, or take a wrong turn? How much would it be worth to you if you could see problems before they came so that you could take evasive action? That's exactly what the Word of God will do. In keeping God's Word there is great reward!

Keep on Planting

I encourage you to take the Word of God and center your life around it. Meditate on the Word day and night. As you do, the Word will cause change to come in your life effortlessly. It will be automatic. As you renew your mind to God's Word, you too will begin to prove—make manifest to your physical senses—God's good, acceptable, and perfect will.

If you aren't experiencing the abundance and victory that the Lord has promised, it's not God who has failed. Praying longer and petitioning harder won't change anything. You must take the incorruptible seed of God's Word and keep on planting it in the garden of your heart.

Effortless Change

Chapter 6

Subject to Doubt

You will become as you think. (Proverbs 23:7.) The reason most people have the problems they do is because they aren't controlling their thinking. Unless you do something specifically to keep your mind on the Lord, it will naturally go somewhere else. There just aren't very many things outside of God's Word that reflect God—pointing us toward and drawing us closer to Him. However, the Word of God is pure light. (Psalm 19:8.) When you study and meditate on God's Word, it changes the way you think. As our thinking changes, so does our life. That's why we must get to where we're dominated by the Word of God.

When John the Baptist had doubts, Jesus pointed him to the Word of God to overcome them. (See Luke 7:18-23.) This is simple, but so profound. And yet, not many people believe this truth.

Personal Responsibility

I'm not one of those ministers who sneaks in and walks up to the stage after the praise and worship is nearly over. I talk to lots of people before and after the meetings. At our meetings, I'll spend two or three hours in personal ministry to people on a one-to-one basis, outside of my preaching in the service. I know by dealing firsthand with hundreds of people on a regular basis that many folks are struggling. They have doubt and fear. The doctor told them they're going to die, and they want me to help them overcome. They want me to wave my hand over them to take away their fears. They're looking to me to impart healing to them. I'm not saying that I can't help people. However, it's wrong for us to look to another human being for our help.

When John the Baptist had doubts, Jesus didn't just say, "Oh, John. I know how you feel. I'm going to take care of this for you. I'll handle it from here." The Lord didn't just wave His hand and then John was free of doubt and guilt. That's not at all what happened. Jesus referred John back to the Word of God.

If you would just take God's Word and use it yourself, you wouldn't have to follow people around from meeting to meeting begging others to pray for you. Don't take what I'm saying out of context. I'm not against you having someone else pray for you. It takes time to get into the Word of God and start seeing the life that's in the Word released into your life. During that period of time, when you're sowing the seed and waiting for it to increase and grow to the point that it will bring liberty in your life, don't be so stubborn or proud that you won't go to someone for help and ask them to pray for you.

But don't be one of those people who just refuse to take personal responsibility. These people don't get into the Word of God for themselves and let it transform them, nor do they have any plans for doing so in the future. Their life is just occupied with work, pleasures, or other distractions. They have no intention of making the Word of God a central part of their life. Like many others, they try, instead, to allow someone like me or another pastor to do their seeking of the Lord for them. That's just not going to work.

Now, while you're in the process of seeking the Lord, growing to maturity, and getting the Word of God working in you, don't be too proud to ask for help if you come into a problem. But don't be someone who isn't even trying, who doesn't even have a desire to try to get into the Word for themself. If your life is too busy to be in the Word of God, and you're just trying to bootleg the Gospel off of me or someone else, it's not going to work.

If you like to watch my television program or listen to my radio show, I'm glad. I'm not against anybody else's program, or Christian programming in general. It has been a real blessing from the Lord in many people's lives. However, if all you're doing is receiving your nourishment from God after it's already been digested by someone else, you aren't going to grow much. If you aren't going to take the Word firsthand, then you aren't going to mature.

Absolutely Committed

The Lord dealt with John the Baptist when he had doubt by referring him back to the Word of God. He didn't just take care of it for him. He didn't wave His hand and solve the problem. Jesus told John to go back to the Word of God.

> *Now when John had heard in the prison the works of Christ, he sent two of his disciples, And said unto him, Art thou he that should come, or do we look for another?*
>
> *Matthew 11:2–3*

John the Baptist was a man who was mightily used of God. He is the only person in the Bible—Old or New Testament—who was baptized in the Holy Spirit while he was still in his mother's womb. (Luke 1:15.) Before he was physically born, he was filled with the Holy Spirit. John was a unique character, mightily anointed and blessed by God.

John spent thirty years in the desert preparing for his ministry. He never experienced the normal things that people go through. He was totally focused on his calling. Then he burst upon the scene, and in six months' time he turned not only the Jewish nation, but also all of the nations surrounding Israel to an expectancy of the Messiah's coming. John saw the greatest revival that had ever happened in history up until that time, possibly the greatest revival that's ever taken place anywhere. This was the man who began it.

At one time, John was absolutely certain that Jesus was the Messiah. He sent his own disciples off after Christ saying, "He must increase, but I must decrease" (John 3:30). The Pharisees came out to John and tried to make him envious of Jesus by saying, "Don't you realize that Jesus now has more disciples than you? He's baptized more people than you." Instead of becoming envious, John responded by saying, "I'm not even worthy to stoop over and undo His sandals." (See John 1:24-27.) John knew his place. John knew who Jesus was, and he was absolutely committed to Him.

Fireball on Ice

But John's confidence began to waiver after being in prison for an unspecified amount of time. He had been in prison a minimum of six months—possibly as long as two years—this fireball for God had been put on ice. John had been forbidden to communicate with his followers or influence people. After such a long period of time, this hardship began to wear on him.

So when John the Baptist sent two of his remaining disciples to inquire if Jesus was the Messiah or if he should look for another, keep in mind this wasn't some newcomer to the Lord who was asking this question. This was someone who had this question answered before. This was the man who knew beyond a shadow of a doubt at one time that Jesus was the Christ. Yet in the midst of these struggles, here he was doubting that Jesus was the Messiah.

> *Art thou he that should come, or do we look for another?*
> *Matthew 11:3*

This is nothing but pure doubt! This was a major problem on John the Baptist's part because at one time he had been absolutely certain of who Jesus was. He had even been given a sign from God confirming that Jesus was the promised Messiah.

> *Jesus, when he was baptized, went up straightway out of the water: and, lo, the heavens were opened unto him, and he saw the Spirit of God descending like a dove, and lighting upon him: And lo a voice from heaven, saying, This is my beloved Son, in whom I am well pleased.*
> *Matthew 3:16-17*

> *And the Holy Ghost descended in a bodily shape like a dove upon him, and a voice came from heaven, which said, Thou art my beloved Son; in thee I am well pleased.*
> *Luke 3:22*

God told John that the one upon whom he saw the Spirit of God descend in the shape of a dove and remain on Him would be the Messiah. (See John 1:33.) John the Baptist received this visible sign when he baptized Jesus in water and the Holy Spirit descended in the form of a dove. He also heard an audible voice from heaven saying, "This is my beloved Son, in whom I am well pleased" (Matthew 3:17). John not only had the scriptures and the witness in his own heart, but he also had an audible and visible sign.

Hope Deferred

What do you need to be able to believe? That's a really good question. Some people think, *If I was one of Jesus' twelve disciples, I wouldn't struggle with doubt. If I could see a vision, if I had a tangible tingling in my hands, if I could hear an audible voice from God—then I would believe.* John had every one of those things and yet, here he was doubting.

It doesn't matter who you are or how strong your faith has been, every one of us is capable of doubt. When you get put in a negative situation over a long period of time, the tendency is to doubt. Negative circumstances tend to just beat faith out of you and cause doubt to come.

That's exactly what happened with John the Baptist. He had been in prison for at least six months, possibly as long as two years by this time. John had been a stark raving mad fanatic of God. He was bold, wild, and fearless. John pronounced judgment against Herod because he had taken his brother's wife while his brother was still alive and made her his wife. (See Matthew 14:3-4.) It was an ungodly alliance, and John risked everything speaking the truth about it. In time, his boldness cost him his life. He was imprisoned because of it, and then killed.

John was fearless in proclaiming what was right and wrong. He lived to speak God's truth and see people change. Once he came on the scene, his preaching changed an entire nation in six months' time. John was a high-energy guy who just loved to be in the center of it all speaking forth God's Word. He was a bony-fingered prophet. That's the way John was. Yet now we see him silenced and put in prison. Sure, he probably talked to the prison guards about God, but he was kept physically restrained from being able to continue to fulfill his ministry.

Proverbs 13:12 reveals that:

Hope deferred maketh the heart sick.

John the Baptist's hope was to be out there preaching the Gospel, preparing the way for the Lord, and turning people to Him. Yet, it just wasn't coming to pass. So this began to wear on him.

The Church Age

Another important factor that contributed to John the Baptist's doubt was the misunderstanding of what Messiah would do when He came. During the time of Jesus, the people didn't have a clear understanding that the coming of the Lord would take place in two Advents, as we call it. The first coming of Jesus culminated in His crucifixion, resurrection, and ascension. Since then, there's been this intervening period of time of more than 2,000 years which we call the "Church Age." Today, believers everywhere continue to look forward to the second coming of the Lord. (Revelation 22:20.)

All of this was prophesied in the Old Testament, but it all ran together in the people's minds. Take for instance Isaiah 61:1-2, which Jesus quoted in Luke 4, saying:

The Spirit of the Lord is upon me, because he hath anointed
me to preach the gospel to the poor; he hath sent me to heal
the brokenhearted, to preach deliverance to the captives, and
recovering of sight to the blind, to set at liberty them that are
bruised, To preach the acceptable year of the Lord.

Luke 4:18-19

This was definitely a prophecy of the Messiah that was fulfilled when Jesus came to this earth in His first Advent. Jesus did, was doing, and would later do all of these things. He Himself declared:

This day is this scripture fulfilled in your ears.

Luke 4:21

Yet in comparing Luke 4:18-19 with Isaiah 61:1-2, notice how the Lord stopped right before completing verse 2, which says:

To proclaim the acceptable year of the LORD, and the day of
vengeance of our God.

Why did Jesus stop before proclaiming the day of vengeance of our God? Because that portion of the prophecy about Him will come to pass at His second coming, when He brings judgment to the earth. You can see that if you just read the Old Testament scripture without the benefit of the New Testament commentary, it would be easy to run these things together.

Heartsick

All of these Old Testament prophecies concerning the Messiah gave the impression that the first and second comings of Jesus would take place as one event. People didn't clearly understand that there would be two Advents. Due to this, the people of Jesus' time eagerly anticipated that the Lord would not only come and reconcile us back to God, but that He would also put down Roman rule, institute the kingdom of God, judge the ungodly, and physically rule on the earth. That's what they were expecting.

Personally, I believe that John the Baptist was of the same opinion, which was one of the reasons that he began to doubt that Jesus was indeed the Christ. At one time, John had no doubt. He'd heard an audible voice and seen a visible sign, but things weren't playing out the way he thought they would. He thought that if Jesus truly was the promised Messiah, He would have come and destroyed the Romans. He thought Jesus would have come and taken him out of prison. He thought Jesus would have ushered in the kingdom of God and begun to physically rule upon this earth. Those things weren't happening. It could have been up to two or two and a half years' time since John had baptized Him, but Jesus still hadn't yet made a political statement. He hadn't tried to reform society. Jesus was simply speaking to individuals about their personal relationship to God.

"Hope deferred maketh the heart sick" (Proverbs 13:12). If John the Baptist's hope wasn't right on, this negative experience could have caused his heart to sink. If he was like almost everybody else in scripture, he too was wondering:

Lord, wilt thou at this time restore again the kingdom to Israel?

Acts 1:6

If John the Baptist didn't have a clear understanding that there was going to be this Church Age intervening between the first and second comings of the Lord, then these negative circumstances could have caused his heart to become sick.

John wasn't seeing his hope for the kingdom of God coming to pass. He was locked up in prison and couldn't minister anymore. Prisons in those days were horrible places. Yet not being able to fulfill your God-given calling can be even more frustrating and discouraging than physical imprisonment. It's obvious that all of these negative circumstances worked together to cause John the Baptist to go back and reconsider, "Have I heard from God correctly? Did I miss Him?"

If you're in negative circumstances, if your hope has been deferred and you aren't seeing things come to pass the way you thought you should, you could also fall into this same trap. Jesus Himself said that John the Baptist was the greatest man that had ever lived on the face of the earth up until this time. (See Matthew 11:11; Luke 7:28.) John the Baptist was the greatest man who had ever lived, yet even he was subject to doubt. When he got into a high-pressure situation, he began to doubt even the things that had been so emphatically confirmed to him. This just shows us that anybody is capable of doubt.

Subject to Doubt

Maintain Thrust

In your Christian life, you must maintain your seeking of the Lord. You can't just turn off the engine and coast. Like an airplane, you must maintain that thrust in order to be able to maintain your lift. A helicopter has the aerodynamics of a rock if you turn the engine off and the blades quit turning. It's going to fall. You must maintain that power and lift in order to overcome gravity and fly.

All of us are subject to doubt. John the Baptist was a man who had been filled with the Holy Spirit before he was even born. He was a man who walked with God constantly, who caused the greatest revival in the history of the world. John had an audible and visible sign from God and at one time had no doubt whatsoever about who Jesus truly was. If negative pressures and circumstances could make someone like that,over a period of time, doubt, it can happen to you.

Are you someone who only seeks God every once in awhile? Do you just seek Him when your back is against the wall so that you can receive deliverance and then go back to your carnal ways? We need to be on guard and watchful. We need to recognize that unbelief is like gravity—it's always pulling. It never turns off. You can rise above unbelief by applying the power of God in your life, but you can't just turn your faith engine off and coast. The moment you start coasting, you're coming down. You may float and go further than someone else, but the moment you switch off that power of faith, you're headed down.

If John the Baptist could doubt, you can doubt. You need to maintain your focus on the Lord, and resist—actively fight against—doubt. (James 4:7.)

Chapter 7

A Crisis Situation

As John the Baptist wrestled with doubt, he sent two of his disciples to Jesus to ask if He really was the Christ. (Matthew 11:2-3.)

> *Jesus answered and said unto them, Go and shew John again those things which ye do hear and see: The blind receive their sight, and the lame walk, the lepers are cleansed, and the deaf hear, the dead are raised up, and the poor have the gospel preached to them. And blessed is he, whosoever shall not be offended in me.*
>
> *Matthew 11:4-6*

Luke's account of this same event, found in Luke 7:18-23, adds a minor detail that makes all the difference in the world, but before we look into this further, I'd like to encourage you to check out my *Life for Today Study Bible and Commentary – Gospels Edition.* This hardbound book has over six hundred pages containing all four Gospels in their entirety, commentary, cross-references, footnotes, and other great study tools. In addition to all this, one unique and very important feature is that the four Gospel accounts are organized chronologically, event by event. This means that all the scriptures in Matthew, Mark, Luke, and John concerning each

Gospel incident have been conveniently laid out together on one page. This allows you to gain a comparative understanding of the Gospels and see the slight differences of recorded details that shed important additional light on certain events that you wouldn't normally see by just reading them apart from each other. By putting the exact same story, as recorded by the different Gospel authors, together side by side, you can see noticeable differences. Nothing contradicts. They just add new information to paint a fuller picture of what actually happened. Whether you use the *Life for Today Study Bible and Commentary – Gospels Edition* for devotional and/or study purposes, it would be a worthwhile investment and powerful addition to your spiritual tool belt.

A Fuller Picture

After John the Baptist's disciples asked Jesus John's question, Luke's account paints a fuller picture of the scene and Christ's response by saying:

> *And in that same hour he cured many of their infirmities and plagues, and of evil spirits; and unto many that were blind he gave sight. Then Jesus answering said unto them, Go your way, and tell John what things ye have seen and heard; how that the blind see, the lame walk, the lepers are cleansed, the deaf hear, the dead are raised, to the poor the gospel is preached.*
>
> *Luke 7:21-22*

Matthew's account of this instance simply recorded John's disciples asking their question and Jesus' answer to them. (Matthew

11:2-6.) However, here in Luke's account we see that before Jesus answered John the Baptist's disciples:

> *In that same hour he cured many of their infirmities and*
> *plagues, and of evil spirits; and unto many that were blind*
> *he gave sight.*
>
> *Luke 7:21*

"In that same hour" implies that for nearly an hour after the question had been asked, Jesus didn't answer John the Baptist's disciples, but He performed all of these healings and miracles. Then He told these disciples to go back and tell John the Baptist what they had just seen and heard. That's a major difference from Matthew's account where it seems like Jesus immediately answered their question with the words, "Go back and tell him what you have seen and heard."

Notice how specific Luke was in mentioning each type of miracle Jesus performed. Later on we'll see just how important this was. But for now, just recognize that Jesus spent about an hour performing all these miracles before telling John's disciples to go back and tell him all that they'd seen and heard.

Out of Earshot

> *And as they [John's disciples] departed, Jesus began to say*
> *unto the multitudes concerning John...*
>
> *Matthew 11:7 (brackets mine)*

Effortless Change

Luke's account records this scene slightly differently, saying:

And when the messengers of John were [past tense] departed,
he began to speak unto the people concerning John...
                                Luke 7:24 (brackets mine)

Instead of "as they departed," Jesus actually waited until *after* John the Baptist's disciples had already departed before He started saying all these complimentary things about him.

By comparing both Matthew and Luke's two accounts of this one incidence, we can see that Jesus didn't even answer John the Baptist's disciples for about an hour's period of time. Instead of giving them a straight answer right away, what He did was go out and open up blind eyes, raise people from the dead, cast demons out of folks, and cause the lame to walk and the deaf to hear. He did all of these miracles in the period of one hour!

I've seen blind eyes opened, people raised from the dead, and folks come out of wheelchairs. I've seen many miracles happen, but I've never seen all of that happen in the period of one hour. I've seen multiple miracles within a short period of time, but the Lord crammed raising people from the dead, blind eyes opening, deaf ears hearing, and the lame walking all in one hour. Imagine the impact this would have had on you!

Then, after John the Baptist's disciples were out of earshot so they couldn't bring back to him what Jesus was about to say because they were already gone, the Lord began to say these things that—at least to my way of thinking—would have actually been more beneficial to John than the answer Jesus gave John's disciples.

A Crisis Situation

In John's Shoes

Put yourself in John's shoes. You are one of the central figures in the nation. People looked to you for leadership. At one time, hundreds of thousands of people said that you were the most important figure in the entire nation. You had that kind of a following. Now here you are, in your darkest crisis hour, doubting the very truths that made you the instrument that God had used in such a mighty way. You're at your lowest. In prison, it looks like you are going to be executed at any time. (As it turned out, John the Baptist was beheaded – see Matthew 14:3-12.)

During this low period of time, you send word to the person who has taken your place and succeeded you. This is the same person whom you promoted and actually pushed to the forefront. You're the one who drew all of the crowds, but then you told them to follow Him. You drew all the people together and then turned them over to Him. In your crisis moment, you send to Jesus asking for help, but it didn't even seem like the Lord helped your disciples at first. He ignored them and performed these miracles. Then He told them:

Go your way, and tell John what things ye have seen and heard; how that the blind see, the lame walk, the lepers are cleansed, the deaf hear, the dead are raised, to the poor the gospel is preached. And blessed is he, whosoever shall not be offended in me.

Luke 7:22-23

When I first read these passages of scripture, I actually felt sorry for John. I thought, *Jesus didn't really do much to help John the Baptist here.* Think about it. John the Baptist had been separated to the

67

Gospel from his mother's womb. He didn't have a normal childhood. He didn't have a wife or children. The Word says that he was in the deserts until the day that he began his ministry. (Luke 1:80.) This means that he had been separated unto God. There was no Plan B or Plan C. He had never had any other enjoyments outside of his calling. This man was just totally separated and completely focused on this mission from his mother's womb.

A Huge Mistake?

If Jesus wasn't the Christ, then John the Baptist had squandered this anointing that was on his life. He had said of Jesus:

Behold the Lamb of God, which taketh away the sin of the world.

John 1:29

John's own disciples had come and wanted to follow Jesus, but they were torn because of their allegiance to John. John said:

He must increase, but I must decrease.

John 3:30

John the Baptist sent his own disciples to follow after Jesus. If Jesus wasn't the Messiah, then John had made a huge personal mistake that rendered his whole life a failure and a waste. Not only that, but he had taken this anointing that was upon him that nobody else in the history of the world had ever had, and sent his disciples, the entire nation and multiple neighboring nations, after the wrong man. He could have been an instrument of the devil instead of the instrument of God that he was separated to be. This wasn't just a flippant doubt that John the Baptist had. This was a crisis situation unlike any other in John's life.

How did Jesus respond to John's question, posed by his disciples? The Lord didn't answer John's messengers at first, but told them after an hour of curing people, "Go tell him what you've seen and heard." Then, after John's disciples had departed, Jesus...

> ...*began to speak unto the people concerning John, What went ye out into the wilderness for to see? A reed shaken with the wind?*
>
> *Luke 7:24*

Jesus was asking, "What drew the thousands, perhaps hundreds of thousands, of people out into the desert to listen to this man? Was it the reeds blowing in the wind?" No, the reeds had been out there for hundreds of years and the crowds had never come. It wasn't nature. It wasn't because the desert was so beautiful. The crowds came because there was a man out there who was on fire for God.

On Fire for God

If you catch on fire for God, the whole world will come and watch you burn.

John the Baptist was a man who was on fire for God. He was anointed by God. God's words were in his mouth. The Lord was giving John a great compliment, acknowledging that he had drawn huge crowds out into the desert.

> *But what went ye out for to see? A man clothed in soft*
> *raiment? Behold, they which are gorgeously apparelled, and*
> *live delicately, are in kings' courts.*
>
> *Luke 7:25*

Was it John the Baptist's flashy clothes or patent leather shoes that drew everybody there? Was it his Pentecostal hairdo or his expensive suits that attracted the crowds? No, he didn't have any of those things. John the Baptist was clothed in camel hair. The only thing that smells worse than camel hair is camel hair when it gets wet. John the Baptist wore camel hair and spent half his time in the Jordan River baptizing people. So this guy was definitely not a fashion statement.

On top of his attire, John the Baptist had a long beard. He ate locusts and wild honey. I could just see his beard matted with honey with a dismembered locust leg stuck in it somewhere. Jesus was simply saying that it wasn't John's hair or clothes that drew people out into the wilderness.

> *But what went ye out for to see? A prophet? Yea, I say unto*
> *you, and much more than a prophet. This is he, of whom it is*
> *written, Behold, I send my messenger before thy face, which*
> *shall prepare thy way before thee.*
>
> *Luke 7:26-27*

That's a quotation from Malachi 3:1. It was universally understood that these words concerned the prophet who was to prepare the way for the Messiah—a very high position of authority and leadership. Jesus was making it very clear that John the Baptist was this man who was prophesied of in the Old Testament.

A Crisis Situation

Greater

For I say unto you, Among those that are born of women
there is not a greater prophet than John the Baptist: but he
that is least in the kingdom of God is greater than he.

Luke 7:28

Jesus said that John the Baptist was greater than any Old Testament figure, including Moses, Elijah, Elisha, Isaiah, Jeremiah, etc. Those were some pretty powerful words, spoken by a Man who was the most significant figure in the nation at that time.

There John the Baptist was—rotting in prison, feeling lonely, and wondering if anybody cared. "What about me? I had a six-month ministry, and since then I've been rotting in prison for years. Does anybody remember me? Does anyone even care?"

What would it be like if you were in John's position, and you sent to the most popular, influential religious figure in the nation asking for help? How do you think it would help you if he were to stand up in his pulpit and begin talking about you? How would you feel if he started saying on radio and television that you're the greatest prophet who has ever lived? Greater than Abraham, Moses, or Elijah—greater than anyone? If you were struggling the way John the Baptist was, you'd probably find such words spoken in this manner by this important person to be very encouraging.

At least, that's what I thought. When I saw this crisis situation that John the Baptist was in and how the Lord treated his disciples—ignoring them for an hour, healing these other people, and then sending them back with that message—I thought, *God, that just doesn't seem to meet the need. Then, after John's disciples had gone, only then did You begin to say all of those compliments. Why didn't You say that while his disciples were still there? Wouldn't that have blessed John more?*

Chapter 8

"Don't Quit!"

When I was young in the ministry and just getting started, I pastored a church in Seagoville, Texas. People were staying away from my church by the thousands. It was just amazing the crowds that didn't come. I was struggling and not seeing very much happen.

I went to a conference being held at Calvary Cathedral in Fort Worth, Texas. Bob Nichols was the pastor there, and the guest speakers included all kinds of big names like Kenneth Hagin, Kenneth Copeland, and others. They were all sitting at the front. Gifts of the Holy Spirit were flowing, and they were prophesying and encouraging one another in the Lord.

There were two thousand people in the auditorium, but nobody knew who I was. I was sitting dead center in the middle of one of these long twenty or thirty seat rows, right in the center of the auditorium. I was literally just a speck in this huge crowd. There I was feeling so insignificant, and thinking to myself, *All those leaders are up there getting words of encouragement. Nobody in this auditorium needs to be encouraged more than I do.* I felt loneliness and several other negative emotions. Anyway, somebody at the front said, "Go around, shake someone's hand, and encourage them."

I had met the pastor of this church, Bob Nichols, once before. Without going into the details, it wasn't a very good first meeting. It's only because Bob is a gracious person that he even liked me after that first meeting. It wasn't a good meeting, and it's not something I'm proud of. Now, here I was in the middle of the clump of all these people. Bob Nichols got down off that platform, pushed his way through all those folks, worked his way all the way down the aisle, and found me. It was obvious he was looking specifically for me. Bob just started hugging me and saying, "Don't quit. Don't quit! Hold on! God loves you. Don't quit." He didn't know me, or my situation. I knew God had singled me out from all of those thousands of people there. In my time of need, that really blessed and encouraged me.

As I read the story about John the Baptist, I wondered, *Why didn't Jesus do something like that for John? Why didn't He say all of those complimentary things about John being the greatest person who had ever lived in history up until that time while John's disciples were there? Seems to me like that would have been more beneficial than simply going out and performing some miracles, and then instructing the messengers to go back and tell John what they had seen and heard and that he'll be blessed if he's not offended.* I struggled with this for years.

Connected

Finally, one day I was just reading through scripture in Isaiah. These questions I had about Matthew 11 weren't forgotten, but they certainly weren't in the forefront of my mind. As I was reading, I came across a prophecy that was given to the messenger who would come before Jesus and prepare His way. This is what these scriptures said of this messenger who would prepare the way for the Messiah.

> *Strengthen ye the weak hands, and confirm the feeble knees.*
> *Say to them that are of a fearful heart, Be strong, fear not:*
> *behold, your God will come with vengeance, even God with*
> *a recompence; he will come and save you. Then the eyes of*
> *the blind shall be opened, and the ears of the deaf shall be*
> *unstopped. Then shall the lame man leap as an hart, and the*
> *tongue of the dumb sing: for in the wilderness shall waters*
> *break out, and streams in the desert.*
>
> Isaiah 35:3-6

All of a sudden, the Holy Spirit reminded me of what Jesus had said to John's disciples, and how He had spent an hour performing miracles.

> *Jesus answered and said unto them, Go and shew John again*
> *those things which ye do hear and see: The blind receive their*
> *sight, and the lame walk, the lepers are cleansed, and the deaf*
> *hear, the dead are raised up, and the poor have the gospel*
> *preached to them. And blessed is he, whosoever shall not be*
> *offended in me.*
>
> Matthew 11:4-6

In an instant, the Holy Spirit connected these two passages of scripture for me.

Just Believe!

Jesus waited to say all of these emotional, complimentary things about John the Baptist until after John's disciples were gone. While they were present, the answer He gave them was to perform all these miracles right before their eyes. Then He said, "Go tell John what you have heard and seen."

> *The blind receive their sight, and the lame walk, the lepers*
> *are cleansed, and the deaf hear, the dead are raised up, and*
> *the poor have the gospel preached to them.*
>
> *Matthew 11:5*

Basically, Jesus fulfilled the Messianic prophecy of Isaiah 35:5-6 right in front of the eyes of John's disciples. He opened blind eyes, unstopped deaf ears, enabled the lame to leap, and the tongue of the dumb to sing. These were the very miracles that Jesus performed and then He told John's disciples to go back and tell John about what they had witnessed. Everything that was prophesied about the Messiah's ministry, Jesus fulfilled in a one hour period of time. Plus, He threw in raising someone from the dead just so that nobody could think that these were coincidences.

In one hour's period of time, Jesus did everything that was prophesied concerning the miracles that Messiah would perform. Plus, He added raising someone from the dead. Then He told John's disciples to go back to him and tell him He had done all of these things and that he'll be blessed if he would just believe. Just believe!

Doubts Drowned Out

John the Baptist knew the scriptures. When the Pharisees came to him and asked, "Who are you? Are you the Christ." He answered, "No, I'm not the Christ."

I am the voice of one crying in the wilderness, Make straight the way of the Lord, as said the prophet Esaias [Isaiah].

John 1:23 (brackets mine)

John quoted from Isaiah 40, just five chapters after Isaiah 35 which spoke of the one who would come before to prepare the way for the Messiah.

The voice of him that crieth in the wilderness, Prepare ye the way of the LORD, make straight in the desert a highway for our God.

Isaiah 40:3

John quoted from a number of passages all around this part of Isaiah. Back then they didn't have a Bible like we have today with chapters and verses. They had scrolls of paper. It was hard to find a certain sentence or passage because they weren't divided into chapters and verses. What we call the book of Isaiah was just all one letter. So for John the Baptist to quote from what we call Isaiah 40, which was very close in that letter to what we call Isaiah 35, I believe it is proof positive that he had to have read those verses to the point where he was very familiar with them. He knew what God had prophesied the Messiah would do when He came.

John the Baptist's messengers may not have understood. They came back to John and said, "Well, He didn't answer our question directly whether He was the Christ. However, He made us wait an hour, during which time He opened up blind eyes and healed deaf ears. People who couldn't talk, talked, and people who couldn't walk, walked. Then He told us to come back and tell you what He had done, and that you'd be blessed if you would just believe."

When they delivered that message to John, I believe the Holy Spirit connected what Isaiah had prophesied about the Messiah and what Jesus had just done. I believe the light came on as John realized, "How could I doubt that this was the Messiah? He has performed everything the Word of God prophesied He would do. No other man has opened up blind eyes, unstopped deaf ears, enabled the lame to walk, and caused dumb tongues to sing—especially not in one hour's span of time. He even raised the dead." I believe the Holy Spirit came in like a flood and washed away all of John the Baptist's doubts. Jesus appealed to John's knowledge of the Word, not just his emotions. When the truth of God's Word drowned out John the Baptist's doubts, I believe he began to praise and thank God.

Victor or Victim?

Jesus wasn't dishonoring John by not giving him these emotional compliments. He didn't just tell him something to tide him over. It was just the opposite. Jesus honored John so much He refused to give him just an emotional response. Instead, He referred him back to the Word of God. That's powerful!

We want emotional things, like somebody putting their arm around us and crying with us. That might make you feel good temporarily and help you over a hump, but it's not going to help you long term. I'm not saying that we shouldn't show compassion for people. However, in the long term, you need to know the truth. You need to take hold of the Word of God. Faith comes by hearing the Word of God. (Romans 10:17.) God's Word is the sword of the Spirit. (Ephesians 6:17.) That's the weapon you use to fight off depression, discouragement, and despair. Yet many people simply wallow in their tears, wanting God to come down to their level and help them by saying, "It's really bad!"

A friend of mine was ministering encouragement at one of our ministers' conferences. He had called forward people who were discouraged, and was going to pray for them. You didn't have to ask this one couple who came up for prayer if they were discouraged. Their body language had discouragement written all over it. They were stooped over, crying, and they looked miserable. As they stood in front of my friend who was ministering for prayer, he just looked at them and declared, "Thus says the Lord, 'Don't feel bad. If I wasn't God, I would be discouraged too.'" When he said that, it encouraged me. In fact, I thought it was hilarious. However, I'm not sure that couple rejoiced over it that much.

Some of us honestly think that our problems are so bad that even God is wringing His hands and wondering how He's going to take care of it. The truth is, your problem is nothing compared to God. Yet so many times we want God to come down and cry with us, saying, "I know it's so hard. I'm grieving with you." But that's not true. The Lord has already conquered. He's victorious. He does show compassion and love toward you if you're discouraged - I'm not discounting that – but God is so much bigger and has so much more to offer you than just compassion. Instead of settling for something emotional that will make you feel good today, but then tomorrow you'll be left needing another emotional fix, what you need to do is seize the truth of God's Word. Whether you feel like it or not, stand up and start saying, "I am an overcomer in Christ Jesus. I don't care what I feel like, what somebody else has said, or what has happened to me. I'm going to rise again. I am a victor and not a victim." Start taking God's Word and applying it to your situation.

> *But thanks be to God, which giveth us the victory through our Lord Jesus Christ.*
>
> *1 Corinthians 15:57*

> *This is the victory that overcometh the world, even our faith.*
>
> *1 John 5:4*

Start speaking the Word, and building yourself up.

Eyes on the Truth

In a sense, that's what Jesus did for John the Baptist. Instead of giving him all of these compliments, He referred him back to the prophecies that he had known, that God had used to call him to the ministry, and that had put him on the right path. At one time, the Word of God had motivated John, and for thirty years these prophecies kept him focused and on track. But in a crisis situation, he took his eyes off of the Word and started looking at his surroundings. He was in prison, and it looked like he was going to die. Because of this, John became discouraged.

As long as Peter looked at Jesus—the Author and Finisher of his faith—he walked on water. (Matthew 14:28-31.) He did something that no other person, outside of the Lord, had ever done before. It was miraculous. But when Peter took his eyes off of Jesus and began to look at the wind and waves, he started to sink.

John the Baptist had taken his eyes off of the Word, off of the truths that God had instilled into his heart. He was looking at his prison and the fact that he was facing death. It appeared that this tyrant, Herod, was prevailing and that he was losing. John was looking at these things, and had lost sight of what the Word of God said. Jesus referred him back to the Word, the Word with which John was well acquainted.

When John returned to the Word, I believe the Holy Spirit rose up on the inside of him. The scripture doesn't tell us what John's response was, but we know that he remained faithful to the end. Eventually, Herod beheaded him. There was no whimpering, crying, or renouncing his beliefs. John the Baptist stayed strong. I personally believe that when Jesus responded to John this way, John recognized, "How could I have doubted? This is what the Word says." Regardless of what emotions he may have felt, he got his thoughts back on the truth.

This truth really encourages me. If I were to go by my emotions, there would be times when I would feel like running away. There would be times when I would feel like giving up and quitting. But I've learned to go by the Word and not by how I feel. This truth has changed me, and it's worked in my life for decades.

Raised from the Dead

I remember receiving the phone call at 4:15 AM and being told that my son had died. We immediately got up and got dressed. It took us an hour and fifteen minutes to drive from our house to the hospital in Colorado Springs. We live so far out, our cell phones didn't work. During that period of time when we were on our way to the hospital, I didn't have any way to check on my son.

When I received that call, I declared, "The first report is not the last report." I spoke my faith; then my wife and I agreed and prayed. We called our son back to life. He had been dead for nearly five hours by the time he returned to life. It was absolutely miraculous.

From the time we got the call until we arrived at the hospital and saw that he had been raised from the dead, I began having some negative thoughts and feelings of grief and things like that. I just praised God. This is not really to my credit, it's the Holy Spirit. He's spent a lot of time teaching and training me. When I started having these negative thoughts, I cried out to God and He started sharing His Word with me. He brought me back to scriptures and reminded me of truths. Because of that, God's Word rose up on the inside of me, and I literally stood against those negative feelings. I didn't care how I felt.

Imagine if someone told you your son was dead. How would you feel? What kinds of thoughts would run through your mind? Well, I had everything going through my mind that probably would go through yours. But the Word of God rose up within me, and by the grace of God, I never spoke anything contrary to what the Word said. In fact, as I began to praise God, my emotions turned around and started agreeing with God. I actually began to rejoice and praise the Lord.

I'm sharing this to encourage you. Even though your emotions are pulling you one way, you know what the Word of God says.

You can come to the place where God's Word is more real to you than what you feel. That's what the Bible calls faith. That's what the Word calls maturity.

Stand on the Word

For many Christians, all the devil has to do is give you the slightest little hint of emotion contrary to what the Word says, and you fold up like a two-dollar suitcase and fall apart. The Bible says that if the Spirit lives inside you, you have love, joy, and peace (Galatians 5:22), but all somebody has to do is just say the slightest little thing to criticize you and you fall apart. Maybe your pastor didn't speak to you as he walked down the hall. You feel neglected and ignored. Perhaps someone said something about you, or didn't give you the attention you need. Whatever has distracted you, it's time to pull your thumb out of your mouth and grow up!

We need to recognize that the Word of God is what's supposed to work in our life. What if you were in a crisis situation and doubting the way that John the Baptist was? Would you be asking the Lord to give you something emotional, to have an angel appear, for a goose bump to go up and down your spine? Would you want someone to call you and say, "I think you're awesome"? If you're looking for those kinds of responses, you're looking in the wrong place. You need to go to the Word of God.

Are you doing what God has told you to do? Do you have a promise from God? Has He led you to move in the direction you're going in? If He has, then take the Word of God and stand in faith. It doesn't matter how you feel, just keep doing what God told you to do. Don't back off of it. Get to where the Word of God becomes absolute authority in your life, and you aren't going to back off of it regardless of what anybody has or hasn't done. When you get that kind of an attitude and the Word of God begins to dominate you, then you will overcome doubt. You'll be walking in faith.

Faith is seldom a feeling. Very seldom do you just feel this surge of boldness. At times you will walk in a gift of faith. However, most of the times when I've seen great things happen in my life, I've stepped out in faith. My emotions were wavering, but I just chose not to go by them. I decided not to be bound by them. I knew what God's Word said, and ministered it from my heart. I stood on what the Word of God said, sometimes with my knees shaking. But that's faith.

Some people think that faith is having an absence of any problems, doubts, or fears. It's not. It's just learning how to reject those things and not let them control you as you take a stand on the Word of God.

Chapter 9

A More Sure Word

When I first began seeking the Lord, I had come from a background that didn't believe that God did miracles today. I had been taught that there wasn't any such thing as angelic visitations, the audible voice of God, or supernatural unctions from the Lord. Those things didn't exist to us. When I became baptized in the Holy Spirit and began to study the Word under the inspiration of the Holy Spirit, I realized that those things didn't pass away with the apostles. I started listening to other people's testimonies, and began seeking to see an angel or have God speak to me in an audible voice.

One of the ministers I listened to a lot back then would often have a burning sensation in the palms of his hands. When ministering to people, he would lay both of his hands on them. If the burning in his hand jumped, then it was a healing God was performing. If it didn't jump, but just burned in his hands, then it was a deliverance God was bringing about. This supernatural manifestation of God's power caused an actual physical manifestation this minister could perceive.

I began to pray and seek the Lord for things like that. I started asking God questions like, "Why haven't I ever had any of these kinds of supernatural things happen to me?" Then the Lord showed me this truth about how Jesus helped John the Baptist to overcome his doubts. He revealed to me the reason that Jesus didn't respond to John on an emotional level, but instead used God's Word to raise him up was because of God's respect for John the Baptist. It's because He honored him so much, not because He honored him so little, that He referred him back to the Word. I began to see that believing the Word of God is actually the highest way to respond to the Lord.

Once I understood this, I turned the other direction and prayed, "God, I want Your best. If it honors You more for me to just take Your Word and trust Your Word than to have a vision, for You to quicken scripture to me and have that be the way I hear from You instead of hearing an audible voice or an angelic messenger, then I'll be glad to go that way." So I quit praying for some special manifestation.

Now, I've had the Lord give me dreams before. The scriptures speak of what's called a night vision. I've had dreams that I really felt God spoke to me. But I've never had what people call an open vision—where you're awake and your eyes are open, but you're seeing into the supernatural realm. I've never heard an audible voice from God. I've never had most of the things that many people claim to have seen or heard. I'm not discrediting them, I'm just saying that I have learned to relate to the Lord through His Word, and that I honestly believe that's God's best.

A Higher Level

Satan can also appear in the spiritual realm. You can see and hear things from him that could lead you astray. But if you go through the Word of God to hear from God, you'll be safe. The devil can't discredit God's Word. The Word of God is the acid test for everything supernatural. It's the number one way of hearing from God.

Again, there's a balance to what I'm emphasizing here. That's why I encourage you to check into my teaching entitled *How to Hear God's Voice*, for additional information. In it, I deal with other important aspects of hearing God's voice that I'm not able to fully cover here.

You need to realize that the Lord may not have answered your prayer in the way that you've been asking because He has something better for you. You may have been wanting Him to come down and cry with you, saying, "It's really bad!" You may have been asking for an emotional response that would make you feel better. The Lord may not have answered you in the way you desired because He loves you so much—not because He loves you so little. It may be that He's trying to bring you up to a higher level of maturity. He wants you to get beyond just an emotional level, and learn to receive some substance from Him through His Word.

In writing Second Peter 1, the Apostle Peter realized that he was close to his death. Therefore, he felt an urgency to remind the believers of the truths that he had shared with them before. This was his purpose in writing this second letter.

Effortless Change

*Wherefore I will not be negligent to put you always in
remembrance of these things, though ye know them, and be
established in the present truth. Yea, I think it meet, as long
as I am in this tabernacle, to stir you up by putting you in
remembrance; Knowing that shortly I must put off this my
tabernacle, even as our Lord Jesus Christ hath shewed me.
Moreover I will endeavour that ye may be able after my
decease to have these things always in remembrance.*

2 Peter 1:12-15

Special Manifestation

The Apostle Peter continued by saying:

*For we have not followed cunningly devised fables, when
we made known unto you the power and coming of our Lord
Jesus Christ, but were eyewitnesses of his majesty. For he
received from God the Father honour and glory, when there
came such a voice to him from the excellent glory, This is
my beloved Son, in whom I am well pleased. And this voice
which came from heaven we heard, when we were with him
in the holy mount.*

2 Peter 1:16-18

Peter was saying, "These things I'm telling you aren't things I
dreamed up. This wasn't something that came as a result of eating
pizza before bed. They didn't just come out of my own heart.
These truths were imparted to me by God." Then to verify that,
he said, "We saw the glory of God when Jesus was on the Mount
of Transfiguration. The glory of God came out of Jesus so brightly

that it was like the sun. Not only that, but we saw a cloud come over Jesus—the glory cloud that used to inhabit the Old Testament tabernacle. Out of this cloud there came a voice from heaven saying, 'This is My beloved Son, in whom I am well pleased.'"

The reason Peter was saying all of this was to tell them, "Look, these aren't our own ideas. We didn't dream this up. We experienced it. We saw it and heard it." He was validating his message, declaring, "I know what I'm saying is from God."

This is comparable to me coming to your city to hold a series of meetings. I could come on the television to advertise these meetings by saying, "I was caught up to heaven and given a message from the Lord. I have a message from God, and I'll be in your city on Friday to deliver it. Be there at 7:00 PM." If I advertised our meetings like that, the number of people attending would increase dramatically. But if I came on and said, "We're coming to your city to preach God's Word. I'm going to share with you the truths that the Lord has shared with me," we wouldn't get nearly as many people to respond as we would if I said, "I've had a vision. God has given me a word for this city."

A couple of decades ago, a certain woman claimed to have feathers fall down from heaven at her meetings. After awhile, someone actually videotaped her pulling these feathers out from her sleeve. Other people have claimed that their hands will sweat anointing oil. Some people have claimed that gold flakes have manifested in the meetings, and that they got them in their Bible. I've actually had people show these gold flakes to me saying, "This just makes the Word of God so much more real." If I were to come up with some physical, tangible thing like that, there are many people who would say, "Let's go hear this guy!" But when I say "I'm going to come and share the Word of God," not as many people are excited about that. That's the wrong attitude. Actually, hearing God through His Word is better than gold dust, feathers, anointing oil, goose bumps, glory clouds, angelic visitations, or anything else. Nothing trumps or supersedes the Word of God. We need to change our thinking in this area.

If you were to unveil two doors, one saying "The Word of God" and the other "Special Manifestation," most people would want this "Special Manifestation."

Something Better

In Second Peter 1, the Apostle Peter was saying, "I know I'm going to be dying soon. I want you to remember these things because we didn't just follow cunningly devised fables. These aren't old wives tales or stories we dreamed up. We have seen and heard the audible and visible presence of God. We were with Jesus when He was transfigured." He's saying all this to validate and get the people to receive as authoritative everything he's been saying.

Peter then added this in verse 19:

We have also a more sure word of prophecy.

Peter had just talked about how he saw Jesus radiate light. He saw the glory cloud of God overshadow Him. He heard an audible voice out of heaven saying, "This is my beloved Son." (Matthew 17:1-9.) He had seen Jesus raise Lazarus from the dead and open up Bartimaeus' blind eyes. (John 11:43-44; Mark 10:46-52.) He had seen the power of the Lord heal the lame man and make him walk. (Acts 3:6-8.) Peter had seen all of these things. He was recounting the things he had witnessed, saying, "This proves what we've seen and heard is real." But then he came back and said, "We have something better than all of this." What could be better than seeing the visible presence and hearing the audible voice of God? What could be better than seeing Jesus perform all of these miracles?

Verses 19-21 say:

We have also a more sure word of prophecy…Knowing this first, that no prophecy of the scripture is of any private interpretation. For the prophecy came not in old time by the will of man: but holy men of God spake as they were moved by the Holy Ghost.

Putting all of this together, Peter was saying, "We have something better than a visible representation of God, something better than an audible voice from God, something better than all of the physical, tangible miracles. The most authoritative thing that we could possibly share with you to validate the truth is the Word of God. The Word of God is greater than any other means for you to hear from God." Therefore, the Word of God is the strongest, most powerful way that we have to counter our fears and unbelief.

Backwards

This ought to be obvious. Yet in my dealings with people, most folks just want you to put your arm around them and say something encouraging. They'd like a little note with a chocolate from you. They'd like this or that. They have the Word with them, but they don't care what it says. They wouldn't say that this is true, but do they come up to me and ask, "Would you pray for me and give me a word?"

I'd have to answer, "Well, you have ten thousand words right there under your arm, on your night stand, or wherever your Bible is. Why don't you open it up and use it?"

The problem is most people don't honor the written Word of God the way that they would honor a prophecy or word of encouragement from a person, or some audible or visible sign. That's backwards, and it's precisely the reason that we have so much doubt.

The Lord will meet us where our faith is. God has spoken to many people through these different external means. I'm not against them. I know many people who have experienced these external expressions, and the testimony of what they heard, saw, and experienced lines up with the Word. I don't doubt that's God. I'm just saying that if you are more insistent, more desirous of a sign, an audible voice, a visible representation, something miraculous that will help you—that's just a temporary fix. Those things don't last very long. Circumstances change. Satan can come along and give you negative signs and such. But if you would just go to the Word of God, making it your absolute authority and viewing it as God speaking to you, then the Word will overcome any doubt you have. God's Word will confirm everything you need to know. It's the highest and best way of hearing from God.

Physical, Tangible Proof

When one of the Lord's disciples, Thomas (often called "Doubting Thomas"), heard that Jesus was raised from the dead,

He responded:

Except I shall see in his hands the print of the nails, and put my finger into the print of the nails, and thrust my hand into his side, I will not believe.

John 20:25

In other words, "Unless it comes out of the spirit realm and manifests itself in the physical realm, I'm not going to believe. I need physical, tangible proof." That's the way most people are today.

Eight days later, Jesus showed up. Thomas was present this time. After inviting Thomas to inspect His hands and side, the Lord said to him:

Be not faithless, but believing.

John 20:27

Thomas answered, "My LORD and my God" (John 20:28). Then Jesus said to him:

Thomas, because thou hast seen me, thou hast believed: blessed are they that have not seen, and yet have believed.

John 20:29

Jesus put the greater blessing on believing because of the Word rather than believing because of physical experience.

Step Up

This may not sound exciting because you look at the Word of God as being lifeless, dead, and dry. If this is your perception, it might be that you haven't gotten sincere and serious enough to have the Holy Spirit quicken the Word to you. I tell you, God's Word is alive. It's living. It's powerful. (Hebrews 4:12.) It's the most sure word of prophecy. (2 Peter 1:19.) A greater blessing and anointing would be released in your life if you could just take the truths of God's Word by faith and say, "I believe this is God speaking to me. I've had it revealed to me by the Holy Spirit, and I don't have to have three goose bumps and two visions to confirm it. This is what God's Word says." If you would get that attitude, and start believing and basing your life on the Word of God, you would experience a greater anointing and manifestation of faith through that than through all these other things people pursue.

God wants to bring you up to this higher level. The very reason He may not have answered your pleas, cries, and begging for a dream, an angelic visitation, or someone to call out your name and prophesy directly to you is because He loves you so much. God doesn't want to keep you on the bottom rung of the ladder. He wants you to take a step up higher and begin to trust Him through His Word.

In 1978, my wife and I, and our two boys, went out to California to a West Coast Believer's Convention with Kenneth Copeland. At the time, I was pastoring a little church, so this was a major vacation for us. We pooled all the resources we had. I went there expecting to hear from God.

The Lord had been speaking to me about making a change in my ministry. I had always pastored churches up until that time, but now the Lord was speaking to me about starting to travel and minister much the way I do currently. This was a huge step of faith for me, so I went out to this conference really believing I was going to receive a prophetic word from God.

There were thousands of people at this convention. We sat way up in the balcony—in the nosebleed section. We were so far away, I'm not even sure Kenneth Copeland could have seen us from the platform. Yet, in my heart I was putting a draw on him and saying, "I'm believing for a word. Oh God, give me a prophecy."

"Why Don't You Trust Me?"

Right in the midst of my praying and asking God for a prophecy, Kenneth Copeland started prophesying. He was standing way down there on the stage, but as he spoke, it looked like he was pointing right at me. I was shocked. I thought, "It worked! God is speaking to me!"

This prophecy basically went along the lines of, "Just do what I've told you to do. I've told you to get up and go for it. I'm going to provide for your needs. Take this step of faith. There's a change coming. You have to leave where you are, and go out into this promised land that God has given you." The prophecy also included some other powerful things.

Everything Kenneth Copeland was saying matched exactly, almost word for word, what God had spoken in my heart. I was just so excited. I thought, *It worked! God is speaking directly to me!* Then, at the end of the prophecy, Kenneth said, "Did you hear that Ed? That's for you." I looked down below and saw a man named Ed standing up downstairs on the main floor. Kenneth Copeland was actually prophesying to him. While I was praying and asking God for a word, I missed the first part of his comments identifying Ed as the intended recipient. So when I heard him say Ed's name, my heart just sank. I thought, *Oh, God. I thought You were talking to me.*

Then the Lord spoke to my heart and said, "If that prophecy had been for Andrew Wommack, would you have learned anything that I haven't already told you? Would you have received any new piece of information that I hadn't already revealed to you as you studied the Word and prayed?"

I answered, "No."

"Then why don't you trust Me instead of having to have all of these other things? Why don't you get to where My Word is sufficient?"

"Father, that's It!"

The Lord was lovingly rebuking me. Accepting His rebuke, I said, "Father, that's it! I'm not going to have to have three confirmations. I know what You've said to me in my heart." I made a decision. So right after that, we left the church I had been pastoring and I started traveling. It was a major change of direction in my life and ministry.

Most of us don't want to just take the Word. We're too insecure. We don't have confidence in God's Word alone and the Holy Spirit quickening it to us. We want to have everybody come and give us ten confirmations so that there is zero doubt. That's not how God usually works.

The Word of God is a more sure word of prophecy than anything else you could ever get. Take God's Word, begin to meditate on it, let the Holy Spirit make direct application to your situation, and then act on it—that's the highest form of faith you can possibly have. That's faith based entirely on God's Word alone. If you will take these wonderful truths and apply them to your life, you'll be transformed.

Effortless Change

Chapter 10

Read with Your Heart

When I first started seeking the Lord, the parables in Mark 4 made a profound impact on me. They changed my life and set me on a course. They actually gave me a track to run on. I knew that God had some awesome plans for my life, and that there needed to be a tremendous amount of growth and change in me, but I just didn't know how to get started. I didn't know how to get from where I was to where I saw in my heart that God wanted me to go. As I was seeking Him, the Lord specifically spoke these parables to me. I still use them weekly, and very often daily. They've become woven into the very fabric of my life.

Jesus taught ten parables about how the kingdom of God worked, all on the same day that He ministered the parable of the sower. This is actually the most recorded information in one day of the life of Jesus that we have in all of the Word of God. You can see this by taking all the scriptures from Matthew, Mark, Luke, and John, and putting them side by side chronologically, like they are in my *Life for Today Study Bible and Commentary – Gospels Edition*. It's really helpful to be able to see all of the Gospel accounts of one event right there on one page.

And he began again to teach by the sea side: and there was gathered unto him a great multitude, so that he entered into a ship, and sat in the sea; and the whole multitude was by the sea on the land. And he taught them many things by parables, and said unto them in his doctrine.

Mark 4:1-2

At this point, Jesus began to teach what I call the parable of the sower :

Hearken; Behold, there went out a sower to sow: And it came to pass, as he sowed, some fell by the way side, and the fowls of the air came and devoured it up. And some fell on stony ground, where it had not much earth; and immediately it sprang up, because it had no depth of earth: But when the sun was up, it was scorched; and because it had no root, it withered away. And some fell among thorns, and the thorns grew up, and choked it, and it yielded no fruit. And other fell on good ground, and did yield fruit that sprang up and increased; and brought forth, some thirty, and some sixty, and some an hundred. And he said unto them, He that hath ears to hear, let him hear.

Mark 4:3-9

Four Types of Ground

Jesus spoke this parable about a man who went out and sowed seed. He didn't dig furrows and plant the seeds one by one. Back then, a person would carry some kind of a sack that would have all of the seed in it. He would just walk through the fields, throwing this seed and letting it land anywhere and everywhere. According to the parable, there were basically four different types of ground on which this seed fell.

Verse 4 reveals the first type of ground by saying:

Some fell by the way side, and the fowls of the air came and devoured it up.

In other words, the seed never even got below the surface of the ground. The birds came and ate it before it ever took root.

The seed did begin to get beneath the surface of the second type of ground, but there was too much rock for the plants to grow. (Mark 4:5-6.) There was so much stone that there was no depth of earth, so the seed simply didn't produce properly.

The third type of ground had a good depth of earth. It began to produce, but there were weeds that choked the seed and prevented it from bearing fruit. (Mark 4:7.)

The fourth type of ground brought forth fruit—up to one hundred fold return on the seed that was sown. (Mark 4:8.)

Spiritually Dull

After Jesus spoke the parable, His disciples came and asked Him for an interpretation. They thought this parable was just about someone sowing seed and how that seed germinates and produces fruit. They knew there had to be some spiritual application, but they didn't know what it was. So they asked Jesus for the interpretation of this parable. They also asked Him, "Why do you speak to these people in parables?" (Matthew 13:10.)

He answered and said unto them, Because it is given unto
you to know the mysteries of the kingdom of heaven, but to
them it is not given. For whosoever hath, to him shall be
given, and he shall have more abundance: but whosoever
hath not, from him shall be taken away even that he hath.
Therefore speak I to them in parables: because they seeing see
not; and hearing they hear not, neither do they understand.

Matthew 13:11-13

People have become hardened toward God. They just can't understand spiritual truth because their thinking is so inconsistent with the way God intended us to be. They're spiritually dull.

For this people's heart is waxed gross, and their ears are dull
of hearing, and their eyes they have closed; lest at any time
they should see with their eyes, and hear with their ears, and
should understand with their heart, and should be converted,
and I should heal them.

Matthew 13:15

Although Jesus made this amazing statement to a group of people two thousand years ago, it's also quite descriptive of our day and age. He said "this people's heart is waxed gross." This is literally speaking of a step-by-step, incremental progression toward insensitivity. A person's heart doesn't just instantly turn against God and become insensitive and unable to hear from Him. It's a process.

Spiritual Code

This word "waxed" literally refers to the way old-fashioned wax candles were made. They took a wick and dipped it into hot wax.

They kept dipping it again and again, putting on layer upon layer of wax until they had a candle.

That's the way our hearts have become. Through the process of being dominated by the things of this world, we've become spiritually insensitive. I'm not speaking simply of ungodly things. Natural things can dominate our thinking, too. We're just so focused on all of the tragedy, news, entertainment, etc., that layer after layer we've insulated ourselves against spiritual thinking. We live and move in a physical world, and not many people really spend much time in the Word of God, in communion with Him, letting their heart listen and learn spiritual things. We become so consumed with physical things that after awhile, layer after layer of neglect accumulates and literally hinders the way that we think.

So one of the reasons the Lord gave as to why He taught in parables was because people's hearts have become so dull. They've "waxed gross." Their ears are hard of hearing. They have eyes, but can't see. The Lord can't speak to a lot of people today because they're so carnal. There isn't any spiritual sensitivity in them that allows them to be able to receive.

Inside of every person there's a spark. There's the potential for spiritual perception and receiving from God, but it must be developed. Since most people spend virtually no time focused on the things of the Lord, they've become spiritually dull. Since there's no way the Lord can speak to such people, He puts spiritual truths out there in parables.

Jesus went on to say that His disciples had a special anointing from God that enabled them to decipher and learn these spiritual truths. This is the second purpose of the Lord speaking in parables. Parables were like a spiritual code. The truths were hidden from people who didn't have ears to hear. To those who don't seek God and don't have a heart for Him, parables seem foolish and they reject them. But to those who have a heart for God, the Holy Spirit has been given to specifically decode and explain these truths.

But blessed are your eyes, for they see: and your ears, for they hear. For verily I say unto you, That many prophets and righteous men have desired to see those things which ye see, and have not seen them; and to hear those things which ye hear, and have not heard them. Hear ye therefore the parable of the sower.

Matthew 13:16–18

"What Does It Mean?"

Jesus was explaining that these disciples had a special anointing. First John 2:20 says that you:

Have an unction from the Holy One, and ye know all things.

The Holy Spirit is sent to us specifically to teach and explain to us things that we can't know with just our natural mind. (John 14:26; 16:13-15.) The Lord used parables as physical, natural examples that people could understand. This was an agricultural society in which He lived, so the people were used to seeing people sow seed. In a sense, they lived close to the ground. Yet, there were spiritual truths hidden behind and embedded within each parable that the Holy Spirit was given to reveal.

Read with Your Heart

The same is true today. Some people ask, "Why was the Word written this way? Why didn't the Lord just record everything He wanted to say to us in a straightforward manner?" The truth is, we don't have the ability in just our physical minds to understand the spiritual truths that God is trying to communicate to us, so He had to put them in this form. However, the Holy Spirit has been given to every one of us to explain the Word of God.

Many people come against the Word, criticizing and saying, "The Bible is so hard to understand." That's because you're reading it with your mind. If you are trying to figure things out with just your natural brain, then yes, the Word of God would be difficult to understand. However, the Bible wasn't written to your head. Now, that doesn't mean it's not logical. It doesn't mean it's incorrect or senseless. God's Word is different than the natural things this world teaches us. It wasn't written to our carnal, natural mind. The Lord wrote the Word of God to our heart.

You can read God's Word with your heart. As you begin to read the Word, you may not understand with your natural brain everything you're reading. But as you come across something you don't understand, you can stop and pray, "Father, I don't understand this. What does it mean?" You then start meditating on that scripture, opening up your heart to listen to God and saying from your heart, "I want to know You. I want to know what Your Word has to say." God—through His Word—will begin speaking to you.

The Rosetta Stone

Perhaps you've already experienced this before, so you know what I'm talking about. You may not be able to verbalize this experience any better than I have, but you recognize that there are things that you now know that are beyond just the words that you read on a page. It's what God spoke to you in your heart. Or perhaps you haven't experienced this before, so you're struggling to understand.

One of the greatest things in my Christian life is the ability to take the Word of God and read it with my mind, yet at the same time that I'm looking at the pages, I go beyond just my mind and I let my heart listen. God speaks to me. His Word comes alive. Life is literally pumped into me through the Bible. If you haven't experienced that, you're missing one of the greatest experiences of all.

This parable of the sower sowing the seed transformed my life. These truths that I'll be sharing with you for the rest of this book are some of the most foundational truths God has ever shown me. If the sower sowing the seed isn't one of your favorite scriptures—if it has not just transformed your life—then you're missing out on one of the most important keys to the Christian life.

After Jesus gave this parable, His disciples asked, "Why are You speaking to these people in parables?" The Lord answered:

> *Know ye not this parable? and how then will ye know all parables?*
>
> *Mark 4:13*

Jesus was saying, "If you don't understand this parable, then you can't understand any of My parables. If you can't understand the interpretation and application to your personal life of this parable, then you can't understand My teaching." In other words, this is critical. I call this parable the Rosetta Stone of the Bible.

The Key

For a long time, archaeologists had been excavating in Egypt. They found all kinds of Egyptian hieroglyphics, but they didn't have a key to unlock what those writings meant. Nobody knew the language. There was a tremendous amount of information recorded by the ancient Egyptians, but it was all in these hieroglyphics that no one knew how to read.

Then one day they found this stone, which later became known as the Rosetta Stone. It had the exact same text written in three different languages, including the Egyptian hieroglyphics. Using the two known languages recorded on this stone enabled them to begin to understand the previously unknown hieroglyphics. This Rosetta Stone became the key that unlocked the entire language. Since then, they've been able to read and understand all of these records that the ancient Egyptians left us in hieroglyphics.

This parable of the sower sowing the seed is the Rosetta Stone of the Bible. Our Lord was saying, "Don't you understand this parable? If you don't comprehend this parable, how will you understand any of them?" This is the key to understanding all of the parables—all of the teachings—that Jesus gave. Christ Himself declared, "This is the key. If you understand this parable, you can understand any of them. If you don't understand this parable, you won't understand any of them." That's powerful!

This parable is a foundational teaching of Jesus. It's something that everyone who wants to prosper in the kingdom of God must learn. These are fundamental, foundational truths that we must operate in and base our daily life upon.

If the scriptures containing the parable of the sower sowing the seed (Matthew 13, Mark 4, Luke 8) aren't some of the most important scriptures in your life—aren't scriptures that God has personally spoken to you —then that's one reason you don't have a clear understanding of the Bible. That's one reason you don't know how the kingdom of God works, and you're dependent on going to someone else to ask them for help. It's because you have no ability on your own to understand. You're dependent on other people who have developed themselves spiritually and learned how to relate to the Lord.

If you will embrace these scriptures, they'll change your life. You may be saying, "Enough already, you've sold me. Get on with it and tell me these truths!" It's not hard to understand the things of God. The hardest thing is getting people to listen with their hearts.

Chapter 11

The Seed

Jesus interpreted the parable of the sower for His disciples, saying:

> *The sower soweth the word. And these are they by the way side, where the word is sown; but when they have heard, Satan cometh immediately, and taketh away the word that was sown in their hearts. And these are they likewise which are sown on stony ground; who, when they have heard the word, immediately receive it with gladness; And have no root in themselves, and so endure but for a time: afterward, when affliction or persecution ariseth for the word's sake, immediately they are offended. And these are they which are sown among thorns; such as hear the word, And the cares of this world, and the deceitfulness of riches, and the lusts of other things entering in, choke the word, and it becometh unfruitful. And these are they which are sown on good ground; such as hear the word, and receive it, and bring forth fruit, some thirtyfold, some sixty, and some an hundred.*
>
> *Mark 4:14-20*

Jesus was talking about a man who took seed and started throwing it everywhere. (That's the way they sowed seed in those days.) As he threw this seed, it landed on four different types of ground. He continued talking about how these four different types of ground responded, whether they allowed this seed to germinate or not. That's what the parable is about.

Simple

The real purpose of this parable isn't to teach you how to sow seed or be a farmer. Jesus simply took something natural that we could relate to and used it to illustrate a spiritual truth. Mark 4:14 is the key to this entire parable:

The sower soweth the word.

Luke 8:11 communicates it this way:

Now the parable is this: The seed is the word of God.

The seed being sown is the Word of God. So this whole parable isn't really about how to be a farmer and get a crop. This parable is about how the kingdom of God works, and it works off of the Word of God.

People are always looking for something deeper and more complex, but this is so simple that you're going to have to have somebody help you to misunderstand it. The whole kingdom of God—the Christian life, your victory, your success as a believer—is as simple as taking the Word of God and sowing it in your heart. If you will just cooperate and let the Word of God germinate, you will change effortlessly.

Disappointed and Surprised

There are very specific reasons why Jesus chose to use a seed to illustrate the way the Word of God works. That's because there is a great comparison between the way a physical seed operates in the natural realm and the way God's Word works in our life.

In the natural realm, we'd call anyone "crazy" who expects a garden to grow without tilling the ground, planting the seeds, or watering the seeds. If you didn't do any of these necessary things to grow a garden, you wouldn't be surprised when a garden doesn't grow up your life. Yet in the spiritual realm, this happens constantly.

People who never planted any seeds are disappointed and surprised that they don't have a garden. They wonder, *Why am I not healed? Why haven't I been prospered? Why hasn't God answered this prayer? Why are my relationships falling apart? Why can't I hold down a job? Why is it nothing in my life ever seems to work?* They've been praying and asking God for all of these things, but they haven't taken His Word and the promises therein and sown those truths in their life.

Many of these people have come to me and said, "I prayed and asked God to heal me." I've asked them, "What scriptures are you standing on for being healed? What promise or promises—seed from God's Word—have you sown into your life to produce that healing?"

They've answered, "I don't know what the Word says. I just know that it's God's will. I believe that God wants to heal me." But they don't have a scripture to stand on. They don't have a promise. They haven't sown His Word into their heart.

Physical Healing Promised

There's benefit in knowing the addresses of promises in the Word of God. For instance, Isaiah 53:4-5 says:

*Surely he hath borne our griefs, and carried our sorrows: yet
we did esteem him stricken, smitten of God, and afflicted. But
he was wounded for our transgressions, he was bruised for
our iniquities: the chastisement of our peace was upon him;
and with his stripes we are healed.*

Then in Matthew 8:16-17, this passage is interpreted.

*When the even was come, they brought unto him many that
were possessed with devils: and he cast out the spirits with his
word, and healed all that were sick: That it might be fulfilled
which was spoken by Esaias [Isaiah] the prophet, saying,
Himself took our infirmities, and bare our sicknesses.*

(brackets mine)

This interpretation in Matthew reveals that Isaiah wasn't just talking about a spiritual, emotional type of healing. Since what Jesus did here in Matthew 8 fulfilled what Isaiah 53 prophesied, it's clear that we've also been promised physical healing through His atonement.

For more scriptures concerning healing, please refer to my audio recording entitled "Healing Scriptures," or to the section entitled "Is It Always God's Will to Heal?" located in the back of my book *God Wants You Well.*

Number One Reason

As illustrated in my previous example from Isaiah 35 and 40, it's important to know where verses are located in the Bible because it helps you understand them better and it makes you more able to share these truths with other people.

However, I will compromise on this point. You may not always know the exact place where a verse is located in scripture. You may not have the address memorized. You may have to sometimes go refresh your memory and look something up. But those truths—those revelations—ought to be yours if you will only seek them and claim them.

When you have symptoms of sickness in your body and you're lying on your bed, ready to puke your guts out, it's not sufficient to cry out to God saying, "I know that somewhere in the Bible it says that You want to heal me." That's not the way the kingdom works. That's like a person who hasn't planted a garden but is praying for a harvest. It's not going to happen.

The number one reason why people aren't receiving from God is because they literally haven't taken the truths of His Word and planted them in their heart. This is why people aren't experiencing the victory they are praying for and desiring, and begging and pleading for God to give them. This is why the Lord used this kind of a parable of a sower and his seed. He wants us to understand how His kingdom works. The sower sows the Word of God. The seed He's talking about is not a physical seed. Rather, the Word of God is like a seed.

If you want healing in your life, take the scriptures that talk about healing and meditate on them. Look up every scripture in the Bible on healing. Study the examples recorded where people were healed.

Tight, but Right

Proverbs 4:22 says that God's words are:

Life unto those that find them, and health to all their flesh.

If you'll take God's Word like a seed, and begin to plant it in your heart, it will literally start releasing supernatural healing into your life.

Psalm 107:20 says that God:

Sent his word, and healed them, and delivered them from their destructions.

God's Word will bring healing and deliverance to you.

I'm not scolding anyone. I'm just trying to be forceful with this truth because so many people are missing it big time. The kingdom of God works from this truth that the Word of God is a seed. Just like in the natural realm, you must plant seeds to produce a crop. You can't have a forest without planting many seeds. You can't have victory in your life without the Word of God being planted in your heart. That's tight, but it's right. It's simple, but it's true. This is how the kingdom of God works.

Quality and Quantity

If you humble yourself and receive this truth, it will provide you with an answer to why you aren't seeing any more victory in your life than you are. It will explain why you aren't seeing more of the power of God at work. The average person isn't meditating in the Word of God. They aren't spending time—both quality and quantity amounts of time—in God's Word. The average person doesn't have a good understanding of the Word of God.

I can attest to this because I deal with thousands of people on a regular basis. Nearly every person comes to me with their sad story. They come to me crying and complaining. And yet, you could take their knowledge of God's Word and put it in a thimble, and it would be nearly empty. They don't know what the Word of God says. They might say, "My pastor said…" or "I believe the Bible says this somewhere." That's not going to get you healed! The Word of God must be revelation to you. It has to be alive in you. It never will be if you haven't taken the promises like a seed, planted them in your heart, meditated on them, and seen the Word of God work.

You're wondering, *Why isn't God answering my prayer?* He's given us these seeds but we haven't planted them! That's like someone praying over their ground and saying, "God, why haven't You let this garden grow?" They didn't plant the seeds!

God has established natural laws, and He's not going to break them. He's also established spiritual laws, and He won't break them either. God's Word tell us that the Lord has "sent his word, and healed them, and delivered them from their destructions" (Psalm 107:20). All through the Word are promises revealing God as our Healer and Provider and attesting to how He wants to prosper us, but to see His healing and provision you must take God's Word and start planting it in your life.

One reason the Lord used this parable about a man sowing seed is because the process of germination is a natural system, not a social system. Social—man-made or man-operated—systems can be broken or manipulated. Most of us have been through school, and many of us didn't really study for our tests the way we should. We goofed off with our friends and waited until the last minute to prepare. Then, the night before the exam, we stayed up all night and crammed for the final. We were able to pass the test, get a grade, and graduate, but we broke the system. We didn't learn the material. It's not retained in our long-term memory. We just circumvented things to skirt by. You can't do that with a natural system.

"I Don't Understand!"

A certain man who attended a Bible study I used to hold was probably one of the worst sinners in that whole county. He was a drunk and a womanizer. He did anything and everything. Then he was miraculously born again and baptized in the Holy Spirit. Just as much as he had served the devil, he turned around and now served God with all his heart. Everybody in the county was aware of what had happened to this man. He couldn't go anywhere—the post office, grocery store, or gas station—without people recognizing the transformation. Because of this, he had many opportunities to be a witness. He started talking to everybody about the Lord. This man opened up his home and had me come in to teach the Word. Sixty or seventy people were coming to this Bible study just to see the change in this man.

This brother had tremendous zeal, but he made some serious mistakes because he didn't have very much knowledge of the Word. He started traveling and giving his testimony in many different meetings on top of all he was doing in his church. Because of this busy schedule, he just didn't have time to plant his crops the way he normally did. This guy owned so much land that he counted it in sections. Each section was 640 acres. Now, he didn't have time to plant his wheat crop because he was too busy giving his testimony for the Lord and being a witness to people. Since his desire and heart was right—he was loving the Lord, and all these things were good—this fellow just supposed that God would supernaturally bless him with a crop even though he didn't take time to sow it.

The wheat season progressed, and it was about three weeks or so before everybody else would harvest their crop. Their wheat was up, had already started turning golden in color, and they were getting ready to harvest. About that time, this man went out and borrowed $500,000 to buy wheat seed. (That will tell you how much land he had to plant!) He spent weeks planting half a million dollars worth of wheat just days before the harvest was supposed to come. He thought that God would grant him a supernatural harvest because he had been out doing "the Lord's work."

Of course, this supernatural harvest didn't happen. When his wheat didn't grow up, and he didn't harvest it, he lost all of this money. He was in jeopardy of going bankrupt. This man came to me wanting prayer. He was angry, saying, "I don't understand why God didn't give me this harvest!"

I had to tell him, "That isn't the way the kingdom works. You have to plant your seed at a certain time, and give it time to grow and mature. These are just natural laws."

He countered, saying, "I know that's the way it works. I've been doing this for years. But I thought that since I was in the Spirit that things would just work differently."

Learn and Cooperate

This man was just verbalizing what many people think. They think in the natural realm that you're bound by these physical, natural laws, and certain things have to happen before expected results can come. But in the spiritual realm, they just think that if they're sincere, really in need, and mean it with all of their heart, that they can expect positive results to come without preparation.

The parable of the sower says that in the same way that there are laws that govern how a physical, natural seed has to be planted and germinate, there are laws that govern the spiritual realm. One of these laws is that the Word of God is a seed. If you want results in your life, you must plant the Word of God in your heart. If you desire certain kingdom fruit in your marriage, relationships, finances, health, emotions—whatever it is—take the seeds (promises in God's Word that speak about those specific things) and plant them in your life. If you will give this seed the proper nourishment and take care of it the way this parable tells you to, then it's inevitable that you will reap the fruit you want. This is so simple that you have to have somebody help you to misunderstand it!

However, most people don't follow this pattern. They wait until they're already in a crisis situation, and then pray wanting God to pull them out by a miracle. They get offended, upset, and fall into disbelief if they don't see the "right" results. Pardon me for being blunt, but that's just as stupid as the farmer who waits to plant his crop a week before it's due to harvest, failing to cooperate with natural law, who then gets upset with God because the crop didn't come in.

There's nothing wrong with the natural laws. You just have to cooperate with them. There's nothing wrong with the spiritual laws, either. You just have to learn what they are and cooperate with them.

If I want results in my life, I must go to the Word of God. I must take seeds—promises that talk about the fruit I want to produce—and start meditating on them. Over time, what I have desired comes to pass and I receive the harvest. That's one of the truths this parable of the sower teaches.

Effortless Change

Chapter 12

Understanding

The seed produces the fruit, not the ground. It's the Word that brings forth the results. This was one of the first truths God ministered to me out of this parable of the sower sowing the seed.

Now, the ground does have a part to play. It can either allow the seed to produce to its full potential, or it can hinder, choke, and stop the Word of God from working. However, it's not the ground itself that produces the fruit; it's the seed.

Dirt

We are the ground. Our heart is where we either allow the Word of God to have its complete rule, or we can let the Word be choked by the cares of this life, the deceitfulness of riches, and the lust for other things. Our heart can become hardened towards God and not give His seed a place to germinate. Our heart can affect the growth, but it's the seed—the Word of God—that brings forth fruit. All I am is the ground. (Genesis 2:7.) I'm just dirt—a place for the seed to germinate. I provide warmth and nutrients, but it's the Word that produces the fruit.

I may not have all of the natural things that other people have going for them—the education, the talents, the personality, or good looks—but it's the Word of God that will change my life and other people's lives through my ministry. God revealed this truth to me through this parable, and it continues impacting me deeply to this day. That's why my radio and television programs are set up the way they are. We come on with a ten or twenty second tease in the beginning where I introduce the subject for the day. Then we have ten seconds of time where my wife and I are walking through the aspen trees while the announcer says, "Welcome to *The Gospel Truth*." And within thirty seconds, you're getting the Word of God. I'm talking the Word, quoting scripture, and teaching what the Word of God says. I've taken this approach because the Lord has given me this revelation that it's not who I am, what I look like, or any other natural thing that will impact the world for Him. It's the Word of God that changes people's lives.

The format is the same in my monthly letters, teaching articles, and books. Everything I put out is chock full of the Word of God. If you poke me, God's Word comes out. Everything in my life is centered around the Word of God, and it's working to produce fruit.

This is the attitude this parable teaches. The Word of God has to be planted in your heart for you to effectively change. If you will follow the instruction of this parable, you will find that change is as normal and natural as when a seed is planted in the ground and grows up. If you would take the Word of God and meditate on it day and night, it would change you. The Word would transform your life.

Hearts

The four different types of ground the seed was sown in correspond to four different types of people's hearts. The Word of

Understanding

God has to be sown in your heart. The ground is representative of your heart. Out of these four different types of ground, only one really began to produce fruit.

It's estimated that in most churches, only about 25 percent of the people do all of the giving and serving that make the church work. Three-fourths of the people just come, watch, and partake of the ministry being given, but they aren't actual players in the kingdom of God. This would correspond directly to what this parable is teaching. Only one in four types of people who had the Word sown in their heart actually begin to produce fruit.

I've observed the same thing happening in our Bible college. About 25 percent of the people really take the Word of God to heart and then go out and change their world with it. Now, many more people graduate and go out and affect the world to some degree, but it's about one in four who have the experience and teaching received at Charis Bible College change their life, and then go out and change other people's lives through God's Word as well. I would venture to say that this is about the same in any organization. It's about 25 percent of the people who really carry the load and make things work.

Although only 25 percent of the seed that was sown actually brought forth fruit, it wasn't the seed that was the problem.

Incorruptible

God's Word is an incorruptible seed.

Being born again, not of corruptible seed, but of incorruptible, by the word of God, which liveth and abideth for ever.

1 Peter 1.23

If you sow seed in the ground, sometimes you just get bad seed. The seed has been tainted or became rotten. For one reason or another, it's lost the life in it. In the natural realm, it's possible to get seed, plant it, and not have it produce the desired results because the seed was bad. However, in the spiritual realm, God's Word is the seed—and it's incorruptible.

The Word of God will work the same for anyone. The seed wasn't the variable in any of these four instances. It was the ground. Now that fact is very, very important. Sometimes, I'll hear people say, "I took the Word of God and meditated on it. I confessed the Word, but it just didn't work for me." What they're saying is that the seed was corruptible—that the seed doesn't work the same for everybody. This parable teaches exactly the opposite.

God's Word is an incorruptible seed. It's never the Word that fails to work. It's the people who fail to work it. It's the people's hearts which don't allow the Word to germinate and release its full potential. As we continue going through this parable, you'll see some of the things that can hinder the Word of God from working in your life, but right now, you need to take this truth, establish it in your heart, and never deviate from it. It's non-negotiable. Never question it. This is just an actual fact: God's Word is incorruptible. It always works. God's Word never fails. We may fail to understand and properly apply it. We may fail to take the corresponding actions it tells us to. But God's Word never fails.

Immediately

As a very young Christian just getting started, this truth came alive in my heart and ignited my faith. As I meditated on this parable, I saw and believed with all of my heart that God's Word would change my life. All I had to do was take the Word of God and meditate on it, and the Word would do the rest because I believed the Word was an incorruptible seed. Through this, my life has totally transformed. In my finances, I'm a totally different person than I used to be. I'm walking in health in my physical body, and I've seen other people miraculously healed because of the Word I've meditated on. In my emotions, I'm a different person because of God's Word. It's changed my relationships with people. I can trace anything that God has done in my life back to His Word. That's powerful, and it's what this parable is teaching.

The Lord describes the first type of soil in Mark 4:15, saying:

These are they by the way side, where the word is sown;
but when they have heard, Satan cometh immediately, and
taketh away the word that was sown in their hearts.

Once the Word is sown on this type of soil, the devil comes immediately to steal the seed that was planted in your heart.

When some people hear that the Word of God is a seed and that if they will just take the Word and plant it in their heart they will see miraculous results, they think, *This is the answer! All I have to do is take the Word of God and all my problems will be over.* Not exactly. It's actually more accurate to say that once you take the Word, commit yourself to it, and start meditating on it and getting to know the Word of God for yourself, then all of your problems have just begun. You may not like what I'm saying, but it's true.

Satan isn't really against you personally. He knows that on your own, you're a zero. You aren't going to be a threat to him or anybody else. It doesn't matter who you think you are or what you think you have, apart from the Lord and His Word you are never going to truly change this world and have a powerful impact for God's kingdom. But if the Word of God ever starts taking root on the inside of you and growing up and producing, the devil has had it. Satan is petrified of the Word! He's going to come against the Word of God immediately and try to steal it out of your heart.

Not Without a Fight

You may be tempted to say, "Well, if that's true, then I won't even get into the Word of God. I don't want to be a target for the devil." I'm not saying that you're going to lose. I'm winning, but it's not without a fight. Once you make a commitment to stand on the Word of God—when you determine that the Word is going to be number one in your life—don't be deceived into thinking that all of your problems are over. They've only just begun. However, if you will continue to stand on the Word of God and not give in, you'll be victorious. You'll be a winner, but it won't be without a fight. (1 Timothy 6:12; Hebrews 10:32.)

Matthew 13:18-19 says:

Hear ye therefore the parable of the sower. When any one heareth the word of the kingdom, and understandeth it not, then cometh the wicked one, and catcheth away that which was sown in his heart. This is he which received seed by the way side.

Matthew stated this just a little differently than Mark. The wayside refers to a place where many people have walked. In other words, the dirt has been packed down and compacted. Instead of being able to sink into the ground, germinate, and take root, the seed just laid on the surface. Just like a bird will come and eat seeds thrown on hard-packed ground, so Satan immediately steals the Word from people who don't get God's Word down on the inside of them. If the Word doesn't penetrate and get down inside a person's heart, the devil comes immediately and steals that Word from them. Out of the four different types of people that the Lord described in this parable, this is the only group that Satan had total access to. The devil could just steal the Word away from this first type of person.

Notice what verse 19 reveals:

When any one heareth the word of the kingdom, and understandeth it not, then cometh the wicked one, and catcheth away that which was sown in his heart.

In other words, understanding is what allows the seed to sink down inside you. Understanding allows the Word to penetrate your heart. It's the door that permits the Word to come into your life. If there isn't understanding, then the Word is never going to germinate. So the Word of God must be spoken in such a way that it's easy to understand.

The Doorway

I'm amazed how some people have tried to make the Word so difficult. I've actually heard of some preachers who think it helps their delivery to chase after all kinds of tangents, and dig deep into the Hebrew and Greek. Of course, there's a place for these kinds of things. I use them myself at times. But some people have made the Word so complicated and intellectual that the average person can't understand it.

Jesus did just the opposite. In this very parable we're looking at, He spoke of something that was easily understood by everyone. They were an agricultural society. Every one of them had sown seeds. They lived in this realm. Jesus took something very simple that people could relate to and used it to teach the Word.

Yet I see people all the time who think it's a sign of their intelligence if they can use words that nobody understands. They talk in such a way that you have to go check a dictionary or believe God for an interpretation to be able to understand what they've said. Some people actually think that this is great ministry. I believe it's just the opposite. If you really understand something properly, then you should be able to explain it in a way that anybody can understand.

I don't know if I achieve that, but it's certainly one of my goals. Many people have written in and said that I make the Word of God so simple that they're able to understand it. They also mentioned that there are some other folks they can't understand. We need to present God's Word to people in a way they can understand.

Understanding is the doorway that allows the Word to get into your heart. If there isn't understanding on your part, then the Word will be stolen from you immediately. Satan will come and take it away. The only people the devil can steal the Word from without any effort are the people who don't understand. You must understand the Word in order to receive it.

Understanding

Digest Your Food

As a minister of God's Word, the Apostle Paul also understood this. He said:

> *To the weak became I as weak, that I might gain the weak: I am made all things to all men, that I might by all means save some.*
>
> *1 Corinthians 9:22*

I try to do the same thing Paul speaks of, especially when I'm ministering in another country or culture. I've been all over Europe, down to Central America, and to certain countries in Africa and Asia. When I go into a different culture, I try to use illustrations that are specific to their situation. I do whatever I can in an attempt to get people to understand.

Not understanding the Word is like me putting food in your mouth, but you not being able to chew or swallow it. It just stays in your mouth, never getting down on the inside where you can begin to digest it. You could literally starve to death with food in your mouth if somehow or another you never get it down on the inside of you.

There are many people who have heard the Word of God, but they don't understand it. They hear scriptures, but they don't have a clue what they mean. There's no spiritual understanding on the inside. Therefore, the Word doesn't release any of its life—any of its nourishment into their life.

> *Wisdom is the principal thing; therefore get wisdom: and with all thy getting get understanding.*
>
> *Proverbs 4:7*

You not only have to have the right information, but you have to have enough understanding to be able to apply and put it into practice in your life.

Satan Steals

This is where many people miss it. Are you someone who can hear somebody minister and it sounds good to you, but within thirty minutes or an hour later, you can't even tell someone else what the person was talking about? You didn't get a thing out of it. One of two things happened: Either the minister isn't ministering properly, or you don't have the understanding to be able to take those truths and put them into your life. Satan steals the Word from you by the time you get out the back door of the church. That's not a good situation.

You need to get to where you have understanding of the Word of God in your life. This doesn't happen through just a casual reading of the Bible, or merely listening to someone's message. You have to focus on it.

A month or so ago, I was teaching on these exact same truths in a devotion time with my employees. I was emphasizing how important the Word of God is. Due to that, some people said that they would like a Bible reading program. So we now have a Bible reading program that our employees are going through. This past week, they've been reading through some scriptures in the neighborhood of Exodus 30. The scriptures talk about the priests' garments, the way the tabernacle was to be built, colors of this and that, and all kinds of things that most people don't really find that interesting. As I was reading through this, I couldn't help but think that some of my employees are probably going to get bored reading this because it doesn't seem exciting to them. They'll just read through it without thinking about it, and probably won't understand it. When we don't understand the Word, Satan just steals that truth out of our life.

Every Scripture Profitable

As I was reading through this portion of scripture, Exodus 30:12 stood out to me:

When thou takest the sum of the children of Israel after their number, then shall they give every man a ransom for his soul unto the LORD, when thou numberest them; that there be no plague among them, when thou numberest them.

Now, that verse might not seem significant to you, but there are no insignificant verses in the Bible. Second Timothy 3:16 says:

All scripture is given by inspiration of God, and is profitable for doctrine, for reproof, for correction, for instruction in righteousness.

Every scripture can benefit us. We just need to slow down—maybe even stop—and think about what we're reading.

As I meditated on Exodus 30:12, I realized that this was the key that unlocks 2 Samuel 24 and 1 Chronicles 21. David had numbered the people without meeting the requirements of Exodus 30:12 and a plague came from God. If you don't understand this truth from Exodus 30:12, you'll read through those other two chapters and wonder, *God, why did You send a plague upon the people?* Then you'll think, *God is so hard to understand.* That's because you don't take the scriptures and meditate on them until you understand.

You can read the Bible, yet because it's not something you're truly interested in at the moment, you can just let it go in one ear and out the other. If you do this, Satan will come and steal the benefit. Or you can declare by faith, "All scripture... is profitable for doctrine (and) reproof (2 Timothy 3:16). There's something for me to learn in every single verse." You can take that scripture, open up your heart, meditate on it, and let understanding come. Once you fit the pieces together, then Satan can't steal it from you.

Spiritual understanding enables you to connect the dots. You don't just have disjointed pieces of information, but you're able to put them together in such a way that it begins to make sense and it starts working in your life. Understanding comes from within. It's something that comes up from your spirit. The Spirit of God quickens it to us.

This principle is true through all ages. Take, for instance, children's ministries. The truth is the truth. You don't teach children different truths than you teach adults, but you do have to reach them at a different level of understanding. You could say the most profound things but if the children don't understand what you are telling them, then Satan will steal those truths away from them immediately. I cannot overemphasize how important understanding is for people of all ages.

Chapter 13

Rooted and Established

When I first started in ministry, I thought that the results were all dependent on me. I thought that if I just ministered the Word properly, every person who sat under my ministry would be totally changed. So I put a tremendous amount of effort into seeking the Lord, making sure I understood the truth correctly, and was clear and anointed in saying it.

Then during the late 1970s, I did a circuit of six Bible studies a week in three different states (Oklahoma, New Mexico, and Colorado). I would teach the exact same truth in each one of these Bible studies, trying to keep the people growing at the same rate and on the same page spiritually. I'd preach my heart out and see one person with an incurable disease receive the Word and be totally healed and set free. Yet, the person sitting next to them would fall asleep in the study and not get a thing out of it. One person would look bored to death, while the next would be getting their life changed by the revelation they were receiving.

After awhile, my lightning-fast mind began to figure out that it couldn't be my efforts producing these different results. These people were all sitting in the same service and hearing the exact same words. Everything from me was the same, yet one person was transformed while another fell asleep. One was healed while the

133

other was bored. How could all of these things be happening from the same ministry of the Word? Then I began to realize that it's not the Word that I speak, but it's the condition of people's hearts that makes the difference.

I've personally witnessed this first type of person that Jesus described. I've preached my heart out, but the Word of God goes in one ear and out the other. It's like this type of person has no heart for or understanding of the Word whatsoever. I quit taking that personally. I've realized that it's not the way I speak—it's just the way people hear.

Where Is Your Focus?

Are you one of those folks who say, "I never get anything out of the messages at church." This may not be the fault of the person who's speaking. It could be the way you're hearing, or should I say, not hearing. It might have to do with whether or not you're opening up your heart and really desiring to know those truths.

> *Blessed are they which do hunger and thirst after*
> *righteousness: for they shall be filled.*
>
> *Matthew 5:6*

Does this describe the way you view God's Word:

> *More to be desired are they than gold, yea, than much fine*
> *gold: sweeter also than honey and the honeycomb.*
>
> *Psalm 19:10*

If you get to where you want to know the truth of God's Word more than you crave food, more than you desire wealth, you'll get it. The problem is that most of us only want this every once in a while. Maybe once a week or once a month we have a little twinge of desire for five or ten minutes where we'd like to understand and be operating in more spiritually, but then we get occupied with everything else in life and that desire fades. If that's the way you are, you aren't ever going to have this understanding. God isn't the one who determines the condition of your heart—you are.

It basically just boils down to where your focus is. If you are focused on the Lord, and you're hungry and seeking after Him, you will be filled. (Matthew 5:6.) But if you're one of this first type of people depicted in this parable, the Word of God just doesn't mean anything to you. You can hear it and it's gone before you even think about it. You just can't seem to retain God's Word. It's not time for you to pray and ask God to speak louder. It's time for you to change your heart and start focusing on the things of the Lord.

Progressive Steps

In Mark 4:16-17, Jesus talks about this second type of person that heard the Word of God.

And these are they likewise which are sown on stony ground; who, when they have heard the word, immediately receive it with gladness; And have no root in themselves, and so endure but for a time: afterward, when affliction or persecution ariseth for the word's sake, immediately they are offended.

Now, before we look specifically into this second type of person who heard the Word of God, let me make another statement: This parable also describes progressive steps toward fruitfulness. The

135

Lord clearly describes four different types of people's hearts, and how the Word of God interacts with their heart to bring forth fruit (or not). I believe He was also describing four different stages toward fruitfulness.

First, you go through a stage where you hear the Word of God but your heart isn't set on it. You aren't seeking after the things of God. The Word goes in one ear and out the other. That's the first type of person.

The second type of person gets excited about the Word, but they don't have root in themselves. The end result is they don't bear fruit either.

Living Off Others

The third type of person gets excited about the Word, and it takes root. The Word of God begins to germinate and start producing life in them, but then they get distracted by the things of this world.

> *And the cares of this world, and the deceitfulness of riches, and the lusts of other things entering in, choke the word, and it becometh unfruitful.*
>
> *Mark 4:19*

The fourth type of person is the one who really nurtures and takes care of the Word of God. They focus on it and aren't distracted by the things of this world. So they produce a bountiful harvest.

> *And these are they which are sown on good ground; such as hear the word, and receive it, and bring forth fruit, some thirtyfold, some sixty, and some an hundred.*
>
> *Mark 4:20*

Although I was genuinely born again as an eight year old, I was a typical kid. During church, I was focused on my friends in the church and what we were going to do after the service, so I didn't really meditate on the Word of God and let it come into my life. I read my Bible every single day, but somehow or another it just didn't penetrate. I suppose it did to a degree. I didn't get into a lot of the sin and other problems that many people do, so I'm not saying it had no effect. However, it didn't have the effect that it should have had on my life. It was like the Word was coming in one ear and going out the other, just like this first person described in the parable. I didn't understand the Word, and it wasn't impacting me.

Then I had this experience with the Lord on March 23, 1968, and I became excited about the Word of God. I don't think you've ever seen anybody more excited about God and His Word than I was. But there was a period of time when that Word wasn't rooted on the inside of me. I was living off of other people's revelation—their teaching about the Word—and not my own personal relationship. Even though I was excited, and great things were happening on the inside, there still wasn't that much fruit coming through my life.

Smoke and Mirrors

I was in this second stage when the Lord used this parable to really speak into my life. It was right around the time when Jamie and I were married in October 1972. Prior to our wedding, and then afterwards, the Lord made this teaching on the sower a revelation in my life.

Effortless Change

And these are they likewise which are sown on stony ground; who, when they have heard the word, immediately receive it with gladness.

Mark 4:16

Now, I specifically related to that. After I had this experience March 23, 1968, I fell head over heels in love with the Lord. The Word of God became powerful in my life. I was so excited over it. I couldn't open up the Bible without hearing God talk directly to me through the scriptures. Although I was excited about it, I was frustrated too. I could see in my heart the potential and what God wanted to do in my life, but I wasn't seeing it on the outside. Since there was frustration and I wasn't really bearing fruit, I began to relate to this second type of person that the Lord describes in this parable.

This second type of person gets excited over the Word of God and receives it with gladness, but they're frustrated when they don't see it bring forth fruit.

Over time, I've observed a tendency among many people to be shallow. Some of these people may be very demonstrative outwardly, but everything in their life is outward. There isn't any depth in their personal life. I don't understand all the reasons for this, but I see this in my dealings with people. Some folks are just shallow. Everything is all about the external. They don't have very much depth on the inside.

I've seen many people in my meetings get so excited over the Word of God that it's easy to think, *This is awesome. They're totally transformed!* But I've come to realize that with some people it's all show and no go. It's all just smoke and mirrors. There isn't any real commitment in their heart.

Rooted and Established

So over the years, I've come to a place where I enjoy seeing people who are clearly being impacted by the Word. They take some time to really think about and deliberate on it. Of course, there are those who get so excited that they stand up, shout, and jump up and down in their chair while I'm preaching. That's okay, too, but I like to watch those who are being deliberate and thinking about the Word. It takes them a little bit of time before they really commit themselves. Sometimes these folks who are just so excited at first don't ever let the Word take root on the inside of them. There is a period of being rooted in the Word that's necessary for you to be able to produce fruit.

Two Terrariums

My sixth grade teacher put dirt in two identical large glass jars called terrariums. Then, as a part of our class project, he planted tomato seeds in both of them on the same exact day. He put them in the same place in our classroom, so they received the same amount of light. He watered them exactly the same every day. The only difference was that one terrarium had about eight inches of soil, and the other had only one.

My teacher asked us questions like, "Which seed do you think is going to grow? Which one do you think will produce fruit?" To my surprise, the tomato seed that was only in an inch of dirt sprang up first. It was probably a foot tall before the other tomato seed even began to start pushing up above the ground. At a glance, you'd think that the plant in the small amount of dirt was doing better. But when you only have a small amount of dirt, that plant

139

has to put all of its energy into growing above the ground because it didn't have any room for roots. There wasn't enough soil to put roots down so the life that was in that seed all went vertical above ground. It looked good at first.

For many people, it's all about appearances. They don't really care about long-term results. They're short-term thinkers. They hear one message on healing and get excited saying, "I've got it! I'll never have another problem." They think it's wonderful, and are very demonstrative with it. However, there really needs to be a period of time where you take those truths you've learned and, no matter how much they've excited you, let them take root on the inside of you.

The seed that only had an inch of dirt grew to be nearly a foot tall before the other one even started poking out of the ground. But within a very short period of time, because there wasn't enough root to sustain the growth, the plant in one inch of dirt began to turn pale and then white. It wound up falling over and shriveling up. It died because it didn't have a root system to sustain the growth.

The tomato seed that started much slower above the ground— as far as what we could see—grew up into a full plant. We had to put a stake in there for support as it began to produce many tomatoes.

T-t-t-i-i-i-m-m-m-e-e-e

Through that experiment, I learned a lesson: A seed must, first of all, grow underground. It has to start producing roots before it produces fruit.

In the spiritual realm, many people don't like the root stage. They don't like letting a truth from the Word of God take root on the inside of them and get established in their heart. They just want to skip all this and get right to the fruit as quickly as they can. Therefore, they don't have very much depth in their life. Their heart isn't totally committed to that truth they received. They may look like they're growing faster than somebody else, but in the end, they can't sustain their growth. They shrivel up and die at the first little hardship that comes along. The Word isn't going to produce fruit in their life.

If you want to be someone who really produces fruit and sees the Word of God work, it's not going to happen overnight. You can't microwave your miracle. It takes time. There is seed, time, and harvest. Actually, sometimes it is seed, t-t-t-i-i-i-m-m-m-e-e-e, and then harvest. It takes a period of time.

You have to let God's Word just stay rooted on the inside of you. You can't back off of it. You must keep digging and looking for greater revelation. Don't just take the surface revelation of what the Word of God says. Go back to those scriptures and ask, "Lord, have I received everything out of this scripture that I need to know? Please show me more." You must let that Word take root on the inside of you.

Failure to let the Word of God take root on the inside is probably the number one reason why people aren't seeing greater fruit manifest in their life. They just aren't giving it time.

Many people know a scripture like 1 Peter 2:24, which says that by His stripes we were healed. They spend five minutes thinking about that one little concept and conclude, "I've got it. Now I ought to be healed!" No, you need to meditate on that scripture, and then meditate on that scripture some more. Spend days, weeks, months, and years focusing on that truth and applying it to your life until it gets so rooted and established on the inside of you that nothing can pull it up.

Depth of Root

When I was a kid, we lived in a neighborhood, but our yard was still a little over a half-acre in size. We had twenty-three pecan trees in our yard. Every year some of the pecans would fall, get stepped on, or otherwise find a way into the ground. Then they would germinate and start producing a plant. My job was to pull up these tiny little pecan trees that started to grow.

Like most kids, I didn't want to spend my time going around pulling up these little plants. We must have had hundreds of them all throughout that place. I'd see one, but I didn't want to stop playing to pull it up, so I'd wait until that thing got tall enough that my parents could see it from inside the house. When they did, they'd say, "Andy, you need to go out there and pull up that pecan tree." That's how long I'd wait.

However, I learned pretty quickly that if I let a pecan tree get a foot tall, there would be about three feet of roots underneath the ground. There was three times as much growth underneath the ground as there was above the ground. If I waited until the pecan tree was a foot tall to pull it, I'd have to get a shovel and dig it up. It would be so well rooted that I couldn't just pull it up. If I wanted to get those pecan trees out the easy way, I had to pull them when they were about an inch tall. Then I could just grab them and pull them out.

It's the same way with the seed of God's Word. Satan would love to get you to where you don't have any depth of root in your life. Then he can come against you and just steal the Word. He wants to pull it up before it ever gets rooted. However, if you grow a good root system, you'll be able to stand despite all the troubles, trials, and hardships that come in life.

Many people are just like this second type of ground that the Lord described. They can't bring forth fruit. It's not because they aren't excited about the Word of God. It's not because they don't love it. They do love it. It's just that they haven't taken time to let the Word take root on the inside of them.

Effortless Change

Chapter 14

Persecution

The parable Jesus gave in Mark 4 about the sower sowing the seed is one of the most foundational teachings of the Bible. In Mark 4:13, the Lord said that if you don't understand this parable, you cannot understand any of the others. This passage is the key that unlocks the revelation of important foundational truths that you'll use every day for the rest of your Christian life. It's truly that important.

Jesus was using the illustration of a man sowing seed which fell on four different types of ground. The kingdom of God is likewise. God's Word is the seed that must be planted in our life to bear good fruit. The Word of God is what brings change.

God's Word is never the variable. It has the same potential in every single person's life. What makes the Word produce differently isn't the seed itself, but rather the type of soil on which it finds itself. This parable illustrates four different types of hearts. The Word of God has the same potential to produce in every person's life, but the difference in fruitfulness is related to how we respond to the Word. This parable reveals that there's really only one type of response that will allow the seed of God's Word to fully produce its fruit.

No Small Stir

Let's continue looking at the second type of person who heard the Word:

And these are they likewise which are sown on stony ground;
who, when they have heard the word, immediately receive it
with gladness; And have no root in themselves, and so endure
but for a time: afterward, when affliction or persecution
ariseth for the word's sake, immediately they are offended.

Mark 4:16–17

When the Lord showed me this passage of scripture and it really started having a major impact in my life, I was still in a denominational church that was against everything I was believing for. They acknowledged that there was such a thing as the baptism in the Holy Spirit and speaking in tongues, but argued that it's the least of all the gifts and not really valid for us today. They didn't emphasize these truths, and they certainly didn't emphasize righteousness and grace. I was in a situation where the Word of God I was hearing was constantly being persecuted.

My good friend Joe, who had a huge impact on my life, served at one time as an associate minister of Kenneth Copeland. He even traveled with him for awhile. I used to attend Kenneth's meetings in Fort Worth, Texas, when he would rent the Will Rogers Auditorium. That place could seat up to 3,500 people. I remember Kenneth confessing and thanking God for that place to be full when he only had two hundred of us sitting down in the front. I was so green in my faith and lacking understanding from the Word, that I didn't realize that he was speaking forth his faith. I just figured that he knew something I didn't know, and that maybe there were some buses on the way or something.

I didn't know much then, but I'd go over there and hear Kenneth Copeland speak the Word of God concerning righteousness. It would get me so fired up that I'd go back to this little denominational church and preach the very same things I'd heard. This was causing no small stir. People were getting healed, delivered, and set free. Good things were happening, but the leadership of the church was against what I was doing. They thought it was inaccurate compared to their interpretation of scripture. So, because of this, they criticized me.

Offended

Notice that this is exactly what Mark 4:17 is saying. The stony ground has:

No root in themselves, and so endure but for a time: afterward, when affliction or persecution ariseth for the word's sake, immediately they are offended.

This is describing people who were excited about the Word when they heard it, and would act on it to a degree, but didn't have root in themselves. When affliction, persecution, and criticism against the Word began to come, they became offended.

The word "offended" here doesn't mean that they quit believing or renounced the Word. I didn't renounce the fact that God still heals today, that the baptism in the Holy Spirit and speaking in tongues is valid, and that the miracles were of God. I still believed these truths, but I became offended, which means that I lost my enthusiasm and excitement about these truths. The fire I had for these truths cooled off because of the criticism I was receiving.

You need to recognize that Satan doesn't have to make you totally disavow the Word you're believing for. If he can just get you to where you're cautious and afraid to speak, where you're hurt and offended and now you aren't enthusiastic the way you used to be, then he has succeeded. If the devil can get you into that mode, he can stop the Word of God from working in your life.

This is exactly where I was when the Lord showed this truth to me. I'd hear Kenneth Copeland speak, get all excited about the Word I'd heard, and then go back to preaching truths like righteousness, faith, and grace in that denominational church. For a week or two, it would be really powerful. Then I'd receive so much criticism that I'd become introspective. I still believed the same truths, and was trying to say them and teach them in the classes I was leading, but it just wasn't getting any results like it had before. There wasn't any fruit coming from the Word.

"Not Your Revelation"

This happened so often that I began to recognize the cycle. I'd hear Kenneth Copeland speak and be okay for a week or two. Then I'd get to where I was trying to say and do the same things I had witnessed of Kenneth Copeland, but it just wasn't getting results. So I'd have to go back and get my next Kenneth Copeland fix. This happened on a constant basis. When I began to see myself start running out of steam, I knew that the next time I got up to teach just wasn't going to be as powerful as it was before. I got to where I expected this cycle. I didn't understand why it was happening, but I saw it happen so many times and that I could recognize it coming.

As I was studying this verse of scripture, the Lord spoke to me. He said, "The problem is that the truths you are saying aren't your revelation. They're Kenneth Copeland's. You're simply saying things that you've heard somebody else say." Before God spoke this to me, I'd get up and teach saying, "I heard this man Kenneth Copeland say…" and I'd quote him. I'd talk about what he taught using his examples, his illustrations, and his jokes. People were being blessed by it because I was sharing truth—it just wasn't my truth. When the Lord showed this to me, a light switched on inside me. I realized that this was why I wasn't able to maintain and keep equilibrium. This was why I was up and down, sometimes excited about the Word, and other times wondering, *What's going on?* It was because I didn't have root in myself. I was living off of another person's revelation. It was a good revelation, but it wasn't mine.

I remember the Saturday night when the Lord showed this to Jamie and me. I discussed it with her, decided, and declared, "From now on, I am not going to say 'so and so said' or quote somebody else and tell people about what their revelation is." As a matter of fact, you may watch my television program, listen by radio, or read my books, but this is the first time you've ever heard or seen me mention someone like Kenneth Copeland in this way. Really, I'm just speaking of him by way of testimony. That's because I totally got away from quoting what somebody else had to say. From that point on, God's Word started becoming personal to me.

I made a decision that I would stand no matter who came against the revelation that God had been speaking to me. I was going to keep that Word in my heart. I was going to get it rooted and grounded on the inside of me.

Mark 4:17 really ministered to me when I saw that the afflictions and persecutions I experience come for the Word's sake. They don't come because of you or me personally. It's because of the Word. The Word of God has power in it. When you start speaking the Word, God uses His Word to bring conviction to people. The Word starts pressuring and motivating them to change. If the person doesn't want to change, then they have to do something with this conviction that they're feeling, which they perceive as coming from you. They may not mentally be able to separate this conviction and understand it, but this is really what's happening. They may think that it's you they're upset with, and so it's you they're criticizing, but what they're really doing is criticizing God's Word that is coming through you. It's because of the Word's sake that affliction and persecution come. People are trying to resist and nullify this Word that you've spoken that's brought conviction into their life.

Revival or Riot

Spoken in truth, the Word of God will either bring a revival or a riot every time. That's what Jesus and the early apostles experienced. (Acts 17:6; 19:1-41.) Not everybody responded well to the Lord. When Jesus' disciples came to Him and said, "Don't You know that You offended these people?" Jesus answered, "Leave them alone. If they're of God, they'll get over it. Every tree that My Father hasn't planted will be uprooted." (Matthew 15:12-14.) Christ didn't take things personally.

Whenever Jesus spoke, He caused a revival or a riot. His disciples did the same thing when they went out and ministered. It's naïve and incorrect for us to think that if we just walk in love that everybody will love us. (Matthew 10:16-42.) Jesus warned, "If they persecuted Me, they'll persecute you." You need to recognize that when you begin to stand on the Word without compromise, it starts to release its power. When you begin to declare, "This is what the Word of God says and this is what I'm believing for. I don't care if it goes against our tradition or the way people have done things, this is what the Word says," God's Word will start putting pressure on people. Either they'll repent and love you for it, or they'll come out and criticize you because of it.

Once I understood this, it made a huge difference in my life. It totally changed my expectation and enabled me to continue going on with God. When I began to get criticism, persecution, and affliction, I just recognized that this is what the Word of God will do. God's Word will divide and separate people. (Matthew 10:34-36.)

"Stay on Track!"

This same friend of mine, Joe, really helped me get started in the ministry. He had a very powerful influence in my life. I remember attending one of his meetings in a hotel where he called me out in front of all the people in attendance. Joe gave me a prophecy that has helped me to this day, saying:

"I see you like a runner on a track. You're running around this track, and you're leading the pack. You're running the race, and doing a good job. But the people in the grandstands are yelling at you. They're telling you that you're doing it all wrong. They're saying that you should be doing this and doing that. I see you getting off of the track, running up into the grandstands, and arguing with the spectators. Even if you win the argument, you're going to lose the race. Stay on track. Get back in the race. Forget the grandstands!"

When the Lord spoke that through Joe, it was so descriptive of where I was at that time. Since then, that's been a word that has kept me on track for almost forty years. I'm not sure that I do everything perfectly. I'm still green and growing. I may be better five or ten years from now, should the Lord tarry, but the reason I am still running the race is because of scriptures and words like those Joe spoke to me, where God has shown me not to let the criticism of other people steal the Word out of my heart.

If I get offended and start to become gun-shy to speak the truth because of what people have to say, the Word of God will cease performing and producing in my life. I made a decision almost forty years ago that I wasn't going to let that happen. I've been trying to be bold and let the Word of God rule and dominate me rather than the opinions of man. It's now become a habit and a lifestyle for me. I am this way because of scripture that has taken root and grown in my life. I may not be doing everything perfectly, but I'm moving in the right direction because of my conviction from the Word of God.

Chapter 15

My Revelation

The parable of a grain of mustard seed is another parable Jesus told them that day.

> *Another parable put he forth unto them, saying, The kingdom of heaven is like to a grain of mustard seed, which a man took, and sowed in his field: Which indeed is the least of all seeds: but when it is grown, it is the greatest among herbs, and becometh a tree, so that the birds of the air come and lodge in the branches thereof.*
>
> *Matthew 13:31–32*

This parable is found in the same chapter and was given in the same context and on the same day that the parable of the sower sowing the seed was given.

I remember one of my very first days as a U.S. soldier over in Vietnam. I was on barracks duty while the rest of the people went through what was called "the CS chamber." It was a gas chamber, and they were teaching us how to put on our masks. They were using the equivalent of tear gas, which doesn't do any lasting damage, but sure hurts and stings at the moment. It's a long story, but I had a very negative experience with that when I was in basic training. Without overstating it, I nearly died.

They asked for a volunteer at breakfast the morning of this scheduled "training." One thing you learn very quickly in the army is never to volunteer for anything. Nine times out of ten, you've made a mistake if you do so. However, I figured that it didn't matter what I was volunteering for. If they sent me out there to fight Vietcong by myself, it would be better than going through the gas chamber. That's how much I hated it.

So I volunteered. It turned out that all they wanted me to do was sit there and guard the barracks while everybody else went through the gas chamber. It worked out great.

The Root System

While I sat there guarding the barracks, I was reading and I meditated on these scriptures in Matthew 13. I thought about how the kingdom of heaven is like a little grain of mustard seed—one of the smallest seeds - but when it is sown in the earth, it becomes this huge tree under whose shadow the birds of the air may come and lodge.

As I was meditating on this passage, I remember thinking, *God, that's what I want my life to be. I want You to live through me so big that it affects millions of people. I want to see people's lives changed.* While envisioning this, the Lord spoke to me, saying, "But your root is so small. The very first bird to land on a branch would cause the whole tree to fall over. The first breath of air to blow against it would knock it over." The Lord used this to paint a word picture for me.

I was more concerned about all of this growth above ground,

which is the way most people are. They want some visible results—something physical, something tangible. They desire to see lives being changed, people healed, and all kinds of other fruit. However, before all of this growth can occur above ground, the vast majority of growth must take place underground in the root system. It's actually the root system that determines how big the plant or tree above ground will be.

If you neglect the root system, you might have a plant or tree grow up for a brief period of time, but it'll never produce fruit. It won't live because it'll never be able to withstand varying conditions like heat and drought. The root system is what enables the tree to really produce and be able to withstand hardship.

This is what the Lord was speaking to me. I desired all of these great results, but I didn't want to take time to get rooted. He told me, "That's the big problem with most people." That was about 1970. I decided right then and there that I was going to be one of those in whom the Word of God would take root.

Seed Power

Once I made this decision to attend to my root system, I actually quit worrying about the visible results to a large degree. Instead, I focused on taking the Word of God and keeping it in my heart. I knew that if I kept God's Word dwelling on the inside of me, instead of just allowing it to come in and out, that it would literally begin to put down roots through every part of my being and the power of the Word would start permeating me. This has been my focus since 1970.

I've taken the Word, meditated on it, gleaned truths from it, and applied my life toward those truths. Every good thing God has done in my life has come as fruit of His Word. This includes the revelation He's shown me, the call to ministry He's given, the people I've seen raised from the dead, the blind eyes and deaf ears I've seen opened, and all kinds of other miracles, as well as the way God has abundantly met my needs. All the good in my life has come as the seed of God's Word has taken root in my heart and produced fruit. Once that seed has taken root, it just produces. What an awesome truth. I don't know about you, but this still gets me excited!

I have some huge boulders on my property. There's one I like to walk out to and sit on sometimes that's over a hundred feet tall (by that I mean that it is more than one hundred feet above the ground). At the very top of this massive boulder there's a little crack and a place where the wind has blown some leaves and debris in. Over time, it's made a little bit of soil. Somehow, a seed got up there on top of this hundred-foot-plus boulder, took root, and a tree is now growing out of that crack. Of course, the tree has outgrown that little bit of dirt that's on the top of this boulder, so it is sending roots down further and it's splitting this huge boulder. There are several other boulders on my property that have literally been split in two by a tiny little seed taking root and growing up. The power that's in a seed is amazing!

A tiny little seed from God's Word can destroy any sickness, any disease, emotional issue, or financial problem if we would just take the Word of God, keep it in our heart, and let it dominate us. It's that powerful!

Meditate, Germinate, Release

But you must protect that seed. You have to let the Word take root in you. You can't go off of somebody else's revelation. You can't just go out there and tell people "Andrew Wommack says…," that's not going to convince anybody. You need to take what I'm saying, meditate on it, and let the Lord bear witness to it in your heart. Once that revelation is yours, then you can go out and say, "God told me this truth. The Bible says in Mark 16…," and then tell people directly what God spoke to you. It's not enough to know what I believe the Word of God says. It has to become a personal revelation to you!

That is profound. Yet it's amazing how many people don't really have the Word of God rooted on the inside of them.

When the Lord first spoke this to me and it became a revelation, God convicted me that I was living off of somebody else's revelation. I remember saying to myself, "That will never happen again. In the name of Jesus, it's going to be my revelation. I may have heard somebody else say it, but I'm going to go to God and meditate on that Word until it germinates and releases its life in me. It's going to be what God spoke to me!" There are thousands of things I've gleaned from the Word. Perhaps I heard somebody else plant the seed, but it became my revelation as it took root on the inside of me.

Effortless Change

Chapter 16

Choked!

Now we come to the third type of person who heard God's Word and how they responded to it.

> *And these are they which are sown among thorns; such as hear the word, And the cares of this world, and the deceitfulness of riches, and the lusts of other things entering in, choke the word, and it becometh unfruitful.*
>
> *Mark 4:18-19*

In addition to the four different types of hearts that the Word of God was planted in, this parable also speaks about a progression. You first start out not having any desire for the Word of God at all. The Word is like water off a duck's back. It's in one ear, and out the other. That's the first person.

The second person liked the Word of God, and was excited about it, but they didn't have any root in themselves so no fruit was produced.

The third person is someone who has learned enough truths that they are excited about the Word and have meditated on it enough that it's beginning to take root. There's a real life and vibrancy coming out of them. The Word of God is starting to produce results in their life, but then they get occupied with the cares of this life, the deceitfulness of riches, and the lusts of other things, so fruit production ceases.

Personally, I feel that in my life I've come through periods of being like the first and second type of person. I believe that I'm moving out of being like the third type of person and into the fourth type, where I am beginning to be productive. However, I still deal with some of these same things I've battled before. I still get occupied with things other than what God has really called me to do. I believe that affects a lot of us.

Constantly Bombarded

In our day and age, we have access to information that previous generations never had. Do you realize that most generations prior to the 1950s were basically isolated? It took a long time for news and information to get around. So people lived in these smaller communities, and they didn't have all of the pressures and cares of this world inundating them the way that we now do. Today, if something happens on the other side of the globe, we hear about it nearly instantaneously. We can turn our television on and watch live coverage of it. It is easier than ever for you to literally take the problems of this world into your life as they are presented in up-to-the-minute detail. Whereas, in previous generations, it would have taken weeks, or even a month, to find out what had happened and by that time, the situation would probably have been over so it didn't cause the same level of anxiety, worry, or care, today we live through crises after crises in real-time.

Today we are being constantly bombarded not only by news and the problems of this world, but also by all kinds of entertainment. We have an abundance of television, movies, and video games. Also, it seems that on the job, people are working harder than ever before. Americans are some of the biggest workaholics on the face of the earth. Individuals who work forty hours a week are the exception. Most workers put in more. People are just pouring themselves into all this information and activity, and it will choke the Word of God.

Now, don't get me wrong. I'm not saying that God wants us all to leave life and enter a monastery so we can just sit there and study the Word twenty-four hours a day. That's not what I'm talking about. However, I am saying that meditating in the Word takes time. It takes quantity time, not just "quality" time, for the Word to take root on the inside of us. Many of our lifestyles today are not conducive to the Word of God taking root in our life.

Sadhu Sundar Singh was a powerful Christian who lived in India in the early 1900s. He saw great miracles, including multiple people raised from the dead in one day. This brother had a tremendous ministry.

Around 1910, Sundar traveled by boat from India to New York City. It took him a month or two to get there because of the mode of travel. Due to this, he had a year's worth of meetings lined up in the United States. He got off the boat in New York City, spent thirty minutes walking around town, and then decided to get right back on the boat to return to India. He remarked that there was no point in ministering to the people in America, that their lifestyle would not allow the Word of God to take root in their hearts. And this was a hundred years ago! Yet, it's the same truth we're talking about right here. The cares of this world, the deceitfulness of riches, and the lusts of other things enter in and choke the Word. (Mark 4:18-19.)

Take Down Time

Busyness is not conducive to spirituality. There needs to be a balance to life, but most people aren't walking in it. Most of us are far too occupied with things other than God and His Word. If you were to ask the average person how they're doing, the majority of their responses would center around how busy they are. When I'm asked that question, I sometimes answer, "I'm busier than a one-armed wallpaper hanger!" Many people say, "I'm busier than I've ever been." That's pretty typical. Yet, according to Mark 4, it's busyness like this that will stop the Word of God from working in your life and producing fruit. You need time sitting and soaking in the Word of God for it to be able to release its power in your life.

Many people talk about having "devotion" times. To them, this means doing a little five minute devotion in the morning when they first get up. I admit, there is some benefit to that. However, if you're just trying to squeeze five or ten minutes of trying to hear the Lord's voice and stay your mind on the things of God, but the rest of the day you are running around at a frantic pace, you aren't going to have the Word of God produce fruit in your life. It takes some down time.

Be still, and know that I am God.

Psalm 46:10

Choked!

You have to be still and quiet yourself. If I get really involved, busy, and going at a frantic pace, it takes a period of time for me to sit down, slow myself down, before I can get to where I can hear God from my heart. It just takes me awhile. If I've been preoccupied with something for a longer period of time—perhaps days or weeks—and I haven't had time to be still and know that He is God, then it takes me awhile to penetrate and break through that barrier to where I'm listening and tuned in to the spirit realm. If I have been spending lots of time with the Lord and am very sensitive to Him, I could get occupied and busy with something for an hour, and just nearly step immediately out of that and go right back into the spirit realm. But if it has been days or weeks that I've been preoccupied with something else, it takes me some time—not just quality, but quantity time—to quiet myself, get still, and allow the Word of God to work in my life.

One night I saw in a dream, "Psalms 46:10." I didn't see the words of that scripture, I just saw the scripture reference. Even though I've ministered from that verse hundreds of times, when I woke up, I couldn't think of what that verse said for the life of me. So, I looked it up. Immediately I recognized the verse as an old familiar friend, but I felt like it must have something more to say to me. So, I meditated on that verse all morning.

I don't believe that verse is only speaking of physically being still. I think it speaks also of stilling our mind and emotions, and there are many other applications. But that afternoon, I decided I would literally sit still for one hour just to see what came of it. It was amazing. I didn't move anything but my eyes. I didn't rock in my chair or shift positions. I was as still as a stone. I had a deer walk right up to me. A chipmunk crawled up on my shoe. I was still.

I noticed things all around me that I hadn't noticed before. I heard the wind blowing in the trees. It had been blowing all day but my business had distracted me so that I didn't notice it until I was totally still. I counted dozens of chipmunks that I hadn't noticed before. There were thousands of ants that, before I was still, I never noticed. There was so much happening all around me that I was just missing because I was busy.

The Lord used that instance to speak to me that the busyness of this natural world limits our perception of the spiritual world. Or as Jesus put it, the cares of this life, the deceitfulness of riches and the lust of other things, choke the Word.

A lifestyle where you are going fast and frantic all the time will stop God's Word from working in your life. Even Jesus took down time. He was in such demand ministering to the people that were coming to Him that He didn't even have time to eat. So He tried to separate Himself and His disciples by saying, "Let's go over into a desert place." (See Mark 6:30-32.) Yes, His goal was to reach people. Yes, He desired to touch as many people's lives as He could. Yet, after He and His disciples had been out on this missionary tour, He was telling the disciples to come apart, rest awhile, and to go over to this desert place. Do you know why the Lord wanted to do that? Jesus did this because He realized that the cares of this life, the deceitfulness of riches, and the lusts of other things will choke the Word of God.

Separate Yourself

You need some time when you can separate yourself from all the busy activities of daily life, and just spend some time focused on God. Now, you don't necessarily have to have your nose buried in the Bible. To a degree you will, because you can't meditate on scriptures that you don't know. But if you've already been reading the Bible, you might be able to just go sit on the porch for awhile and pray about what's been going on during that day. You could meditate on the scriptures God has been giving you and ask Him to show you things.

I do that a lot. I built a trail on my property and I walk on it an hour or two a day. I spend that time just meditating on the things of God, thinking about what He's leading me to do, and meditating on scriptures. We have a little swing out on our patio I like to sit on. You can't see another house from my place, so I like to sit out there and look at the mountains. I just look around, meditate, and think on things. That's an important time.

One of the things that will stop God's Word from working in your life is just being busy. If Satan came in a red suit with horns and a pitchfork, most of us would resist him, saying, "No way am I giving in to you!" Likewise, most of us would reject X-rated, and even most R-rated material, or anything else that is just overtly of the devil. But there's nothing wrong with having a job, a career, and a family. Working your job and spending time with your family are good and right in their place, but it's not good when we cram so much into our life that we have very little or no time left for God and His Word. You may be occupying your life with decent things—things that aren't immoral in or of themselves—but if you have no time to sit and meditate on the things of the Lord, it will stop the Word of God from working in your life.

In my own personal life, God has dealt with me about a number of things. They aren't sin, but He's told me that I cannot afford to become preoccupied with them. I don't need another hobby. I don't need anything else to do, especially with my personality. I have a compulsive type of personality, which means that everything I do, I do to an extreme. I've had some friends try to get me into doing certain things. They're enjoying it, and it's no problem for them, but I just don't have the time to devote to anything else. I have to keep the main thing, the main thing!

I wish I could somehow or another just make people understand this truth because Satan is really using this to hinder people's personal growth. He draws us into being so busy that we short-circuit God's provision for us to change. We just get so preoccupied that we don't take the time to spend in the Word and in fellowship with God. This hinders the change God wants to bring to pass.

Fellowshipping with God

If you are going to see effective change—the Word of God producing fruit in your life—you must start spending some quantity time fellowshipping with God through the Word. You have to take these truths, plant them, and keep them in your heart. Some people don't like that, but it's just the way the kingdom works. This isn't necessarily the way that we would have decided to have it done, but this is how the Lord told us His kingdom operates. Since He's the

Lord, it's going to work the way that He says, not the way that you choose. This is something that I have to deal with all the time. I constantly have to make time and force myself not to get too busy.

Although I'm not tempted to go out and do any of those things that the church calls "sin," God has to deal with me often about getting so preoccupied with the ministry. It's the things concerning the ministry that crowd out my time to fellowship with God and study His Word. The Lord has had to deal with me over that. If I can become too preoccupied and busy with ministry—things that are good and are about helping other people—so that the Word of God is being choked and hindered in my life, what can happen in other people's lives who are being occupied with pursuing their careers and running their kids all over town all week long?

Don't get me wrong. I'm not here to tell you what you can or cannot do. However, you may be one of these people who love God, place an importance on His Word, and want to see the fruit, but are so occupied with all kinds of "good" things that the seed of God's Word is being choked out in your life. Many Christians are simply involved in too much. They're constantly taxiing their kids here, there, and yonder, and they're involved in everything the church has to offer. If you're not careful, it will choke the Word of God and keep you from being productive. These things aren't bad—just natural.

Stay Home

While in Vietnam, I had a lot of time on my hands. I wasn't one of the "grunts," guys who were out in the field constantly hiking every day and engaging the enemy. I did see some action, and there was a lot of danger associated with being on that fire support base. However, to a large degree, it was boring just sitting there on a hill. I was a chaplain's assistant assigned to brigade headquarters. I was on the battalion level. This meant that there was nobody directly over me because I reported back to people forty-five miles away. This was why I had such a huge amount of time on my hands.

With so much time to spare, I just started poring over the Word of God as much as fifteen or sixteen hours a day. I studied through the Bible all day long. I would go on bunker guard every single day and spend four hours praying and communicating with the Lord.

After over thirteen months of just constantly being in the Word and praying, I returned home to the USA ready to go to church and be with other Christians again. Since I had a car, I became the taxi driver for some younger friends as we drove all over the Dallas-Fort Worth area. We often stayed out as late as one or two o'clock in the morning attending prayer meetings, revival meetings, and even all-night prayer meetings.

Although that sounds good, after being back from Vietnam for about a month, I began to recognize my spiritual sensitivity to God was diminishing. My heart wasn't as focused on Him as before. I wasn't doing anything sinful or wrong, but the Lord spoke to me saying, "This going to church every night is killing your relationship with Me."

Now, you may not understand that. In fact, you may be tempted right now to think I'm anti-church. Let me assure you, that's not the case. However, I was going to church every single night—seven nights a week. In the Dallas-Fort Worth area, there was always someplace you could go. Plus, we had prayer meetings in the morning and other meetings during the day. I was so involved in doing all of these things—godly things—that it was choking the Word of God out of my life. So one of the things the Lord told me to do was to stay home at least two nights a week. He specifically instructed me NOT to go out with my friends to a revival meeting, convention, or prayer meeting, but to stay home studying the Word and fellowshipping with Him. I needed to get back into the flow of a personal relationship with God.

Weeds

All this busyness is like weeds sprouting up all around the stalk of corn you planted. The soil only has so much nourishment. Those weeds will suck much of the moisture and nutrients out of the ground, which will keep the seed that you want to grow from really producing and bearing fruit. This is what happens to us when we get so occupied doing other things. They don't have to be bad things, it's just that we're so occupied with them that it saps our attention and energy. We don't really have any time to be able to focus on and fellowship with the Lord.

Honestly, do you fall asleep every time you try to get quiet and study the Word of God? Are you so busy that you aren't even getting a full night's sleep? Many of us are cramming so much into our lives, and it's not improving the quality of it. We've just become busy. That lifestyle needs to change.

Are you seeing the change in your life that you desire? Are you bearing the fruit that you know God wants you to bear? If not, I challenge you to start spending some quantity time just focused on the things of the Lord. I'm not going to put certain requirements on this time because it may vary from person to person. If you go from spending no time to spending thirty minutes a day focused on God—with everything else out of your mind—you'll see tremendous benefits. Perhaps you've already been spending thirty minutes a day, but the Lord is drawing you in deeper. You just need to make a decision that you are going to start taking away all of the things that choke the Word of God in your life.

Chapter 17

Less

There was only one soil that really produced the intended fruit. It's this last type of heart that the Word of God was sown in.

And these are they which are sown on good ground; such as hear the word, and receive it, and bring forth fruit, some thirtyfold, some sixty, and some an hundred.

Mark 4:20

We all want to be this last type of ground. We all want to produce an abundant crop of good fruit. However, the best type of ground didn't have more. It had less.

First Place

When the Lord showed this truth to me, I was just starting out in ministry. It impacted me deeply because I was acutely aware that I was just a hick from Texas. My voice is not what you would call a voice for radio and television. God chooses the weak things of this world to confound the wise. (1 Corinthians 1:26-28.) If I were picking people to be on radio and television, I wouldn't have picked me. That's for sure! So I was acutely aware of all these liabilities—my voice, the way I look, that I'm a hick from Texas, and that I don't have the "charisma" that a lot of other people do.

Because of this, I honestly doubted that God could use me. But the Lord really encouraged me through this parable.

He showed me that it was the seed—the Word—that produced the fruit. And the ground that produced the best fruit wasn't the ground that had more, it was the ground that had less—less stones, less thorns, and less weeds. The real productive soil wasn't soil that had more than everything else; it was the soil that had less.

This told me that I didn't necessarily need all of these external talents that people normally put emphasis on in order to be fruitful. It's really just a matter of the heart. If I would rid myself of the stones, thorns, and weeds, I could bear much fruit. I just needed to eliminate the things that occupy my attention and devote myself completely to God. If I put the Word of God first place in my heart, then that Word would produce an abundant harvest in my life.

This really encouraged me. I prayed, "God, if what really makes Your Word become fruitful is being less, then I can certainly be less. I may not be able to be more, but I can definitely be less. I can get rid of these things that hinder me."

You may not feel like you're the sharpest knife in the drawer. You may be acutely aware that you have all kinds of liabilities that other people don't have. Yet, you can commit yourself to the Word of God and meditate on it until God's Word takes deep root in your heart. You can refuse to allow anything else to divert your attention or sap the strength of your heart that could be going toward the Lord. If you devote yourself completely to the Lord and His Word, God's Word will make you a success. It will cause fruit to come in whatever area He has called and anointed you to minister.

An Asset

Luke's account says:

But that on the good ground are they, which in an honest and good heart, having heard the word, keep it, and bring forth fruit with patience.

Luke 8:15

If you stop and think about it, this whole parable has been about patience. It's been about a seed being planted and then reaping a harvest. Everyone who has ever dealt with seeds knows that you have to give that seed time to work. Time is actually an asset. It's a benefit to a farmer. It's not a negative, but a positive.

When you put a seed in the ground, you don't know what's happening. But if you'll leave that seed in the ground, keeping it watered and weeded, God has made it so that over time, it'll germinate and take root. The crop will come up and the fruit will mature. Time is actually a benefit. Instead of looking at time negatively, you need to see it as a friend.

After speaking along these lines about the growth process and it taking time, I remember one of our Bible college students getting mad and saying, "I don't have ten years to mature. God has told me that I'm supposed to lead a million people to the Lord. Jesus is coming back soon!" So in spite of all the scriptures that talk about not putting a novice in a position of authority, all the scriptures that speak of growth over time, this guy just determined that he was going to violate all of that, and that he was going to get it done on his own. He actually quit school so he could go ahead and change the world in a short period of time. This was years ago, and it hasn't come to pass yet. He saw time as a negative, and had the attitude, "I can't afford to wait!"

Now that I've been in the ministry for over forty years, I look at time as an asset. I've been sowing the Word of God in my life for decades. I've been meditating on these truths for years. I'm still reaping today because of the time that I've invested in the kingdom of God decades ago.

Reproduction and Multiplication

Once a seed is sown, it'll grow and multiply over time. Consider the dandelion. If you were to sow a dandelion seed in your yard, over time that dandelion would reproduce itself and completely fill your yard. That's how seeds work. Time is actually a friend to a seed because it allows reproduction and multiplication.

Don't think, *Oh man, I have to spend time growing, maturing, and letting the Word take root on the inside of me.* View time positively. Every second you spend meditating in the Word of God and planting these seeds in your heart, you're starting in motion a process that cannot be stopped. Seeds are powerful.

It's been over twenty years since Mount St. Helens erupted. Because of the devastation, all the scientists back then were predicting that it would take hundreds of years for the area to reforest itself, for the animals to come back, and for the flowers to return. Now they're just shocked that things are so regenerated after only a little more than twenty years' time. It's far beyond everyone's expectations. They didn't understand the power that's in seeds. There was so much heat and so many mudslides, yet those seeds were doing what God created them to do. They started producing, and by the very next year there were already signs of regeneration sprouting up here and there.

God has put seeds in His Word. We need to take these seeds, plant them in our heart, and just leave them there. If we keep the Word of God fresh and alive on the inside of us, it'll continue benefiting us twenty, thirty, even fifty years from now, should the Lord tarry.

This is how the kingdom of God works. Once you understand this principle, you can take the Word of God, sow it in your life, and keep it there. Instead of being discouraged that it takes time to grow, you can be encouraged. Once you get this system going, and you've invested that time, the Word of God will just supernaturally change you. You'll be changed effortlessly by the Word of God. It'll just spring forth and grow up in your life. You'll be transformed.

I live in the mountains of Colorado. There is a 250 foot vertical rise from the road that runs in front of our house up to our house. Our property is so steep, it's hard to walk on it, especially in winter with the snow. Add to that the fact that our altitude is 9000 feet and it really taxes your breathing to climb these hills. Therefore, I decided to build a trail that "switched back" across my property so I could walk up and down without losing my breath.

I started building that trail by just using hand tools in 1994. Most of my property is decomposed granite and I averaged only ten feet per hour. My trail is 2.5 miles round trip. So, it looked like it was going to take me forever to finish that trail. I worked on it until it was completed in 2000 and still maintain it today.

I tell you this story to make a point. Now, every time I go walking on my trail, I am reaping the benefits of the labor I did back in '94-2000. Yes, it took me six years to build that trail, but I've been using it for many years now. That wasn't wasted time. I'm reaping benefits from that investment of time every day. Likewise, the time you take getting God's Word rooted and grounded in you isn't wasted time. You will reap its rewards for the rest of your life.

Chapter 18

The Growth Process

O n the same day that Jesus taught the parable of the sower sowing the seed, He also said:

So is the kingdom of God, as if a man should cast seed into the ground; And should sleep, and rise night and day, and the seed should spring and grow up, he knoweth not how. For the earth bringeth forth fruit of herself; first the blade, then the ear, after that the full corn in the ear. But when the fruit is brought forth, immediately he putteth in the sickle, because the harvest is come.

Mark 4:26-29

Although this is a simple passage of scripture, it's very profound. It's packed with meaning. First of all, it says that the kingdom of God is as if a man should cast seed into the ground. This is the same principle as in the parable of the sower sowing the seed. God's Word is like a seed planted in the ground of our heart.

Cooperate and Reap

Notice verse 27 says:

And should sleep, and rise night and day, and the seed should spring and grow up, he knoweth not how.

Mark 4:27

In the same way that you plant a seed in the ground and don't really know what's happening to make it grow, so it is with the Word. Mankind, with all our knowledge, has put satellites in orbit, people on the moon, and sent spacecraft to other planets. For all that mankind has accomplished and all of our cumulative knowledge, we cannot manufacture a seed. Oh, we can make something that looks like a seed, with the same size, color, and chemicals. It could look like an exact replica and fool people, but if you take a manmade seed and plant it in the ground, it won't germinate or reproduce itself. Why? There isn't any life in it.

Despite all our knowledge, mankind has not been able to figure out why a seed does what it does. It does what it does just because God created it that way. However, even though we don't understand all of the specifics, that doesn't keep us from taking seeds and planting them in the ground. We've learned a few things about how long it takes for that seed to germinate and produce a harvest. We've learned about what weeds to keep out. We've learned about what kind of temperature and how much water the seed needs to produce fruit. We've learned enough about a seed to be able to cooperate with it, but we still don't understand it. Yet it works. Every one of us benefit from seeds sown around the world when we eat our bread, fruit, and vegetables. We don't understand it, but we still benefit from it.

This is a tremendous comfort to me. I don't have to understand everything about how the Word works. I don't have to understand why just shutting myself in with the Lord, studying His Word, and listening to Him speak to me does what it does. The fact that

I can't totally explain it doesn't keep me from cooperating and reaping the benefits of it.

You don't have to be a rocket scientist, or the sharpest person around. You don't have to understand everything to get God's Word working in your life. Just start sowing the Word into your heart. Begin meditating on it day and night. The Word of God will germinate, take root, spring forth, and grow up of itself.

Everything Jesus Provided

God put life in those seeds. Man cannot figure it out, but God spoke life into physical seeds. He's also spoken life into the spiritual seed of His Word.

Proverbs 4:20-22 says:

My son, attend to my words; incline thine ear unto my sayings. Let them not depart from thine eyes; keep them in the midst of thine heart. For they are life unto those that find them, and health to all their flesh.

God's Word contains His life in it. If you would take His words, His sayings, and put them on the inside of you, then God's kind of life would start flowing through you. You would find that healing, prosperity, joy, peace—everything Jesus provided—are contained in God's Word.

The Bible isn't like any other book. It's different. It's alive.

For the word of God is quick [alive], and powerful, and sharper than any two edged sword.

Hebrews 4:12, [brackets mine]

God's Word is alive. It's different than reading any other book—even books about the Bible. The Word of God is different. There's life in it. If you take it, the Word will give you life where there's been death. It gives light where there was darkness. It's that simple.

Patience

In light of this truth, I don't know why people don't spend more time studying the Word of God. I don't know why we spend so much time occupied with all these other things. The only explanation I can think of is that we really don't believe. We really don't believe the power and authority that's in God's Word. If you understand what I'm saying, then you'll realize that the most important thing you could ever do is just take God's Word and begin planting it in your life.

God has created His Word just like a physical seed. It brings forth fruit of itself. Yet, the Word doesn't work until it's sown in your heart just like a seed doesn't work until it's sown into the ground.

They've found seeds in pyramids that had been lying there for four thousand years. They were dormant, never sprouting, because they weren't in the ground. But once they were planted with the right temperature, nutrients, and water, they started sprouting and producing plants. All of a sudden the life that was in them came forth. That's a miracle!

God's Word has been recorded for thousands of years. If you will take it and sow it into your heart, it will begin to produce.

But the seed has to be in the ground. The Word has to be in your heart for it to begin to release that life. You can't just read it with your eyes and take a little truth into your brain. You have to put it down deep on the inside of you. You must meditate on the Word until it literally takes root on the inside of you. That's when it will just start supernaturally producing.

In this parable, Jesus was saying that the kingdom of God is like a man that takes a seed and puts it in the ground. He sleeps and rises night and day. This implies time. You have to exercise patience.

Act in Faith

If you put a seed in the ground, and then go out and dig it up every day to see if anything is happening, you'll kill that seed. That seed has to be left in the ground for a period of time. There has to be faith. Farmers may not use this terminology, but it's true. The person who plants the seed has to believe that the seed is germinating, putting roots down, and producing. You just have to leave that seed there by faith, and over a period of time it produces.

It's the same with the Word of God. You can't just take a promise, plant it, and expect to reap a harvest right away. You can't just hear 1 Peter 2:24 for the first time, then confess "By His stripes I am healed. I claim it in the name of Jesus," and then if you aren't healed in the next ten minutes, go dig that seed up by saying, "Well, nothing's happening." And then the next day, you go back and do it again. That's not abiding in the Word, and letting the Word abide in you. (John 15:5.)

You must come to a place where the Word is just part of you. It's not something you study for a little bit and then go out and live your whole day contrary to it. I'm not against specific devotion and prayer times, but you need to keep focused on the Lord and His Word all day long. It does you no good to spend ten or twenty minutes in "devotion mode," being sweet and kind and listening to God, but then once it's over you go back to being a piranha the rest of the day—being just as mean, angry, and vicious in your relationships and business dealings as anyone else in the world. You may have planted the Word in your devotion time, but you dug that Word up. It's not working on the inside of you. It's not staying in your heart, and because of that, you aren't going to see it produce. It takes more than that.

You can't just consider God's Word during your devotion time, and expect that to all of a sudden change the way you act that day. You have to take those truths about loving people (John 13:34-35), turning the other cheek (Matthew 5:39), and thinking more highly of others than you think of yourself (Philippians 2:3), and leave that seed in your heart over time. Then whenever somebody rubs you the wrong way, you need to act in faith and let that Word continue to affect you. You must abide in the Word and allow the Word to abide in you, for it to release its power and impact your life.

Yet many people are trying church, trying prayer lines, and trying everything else except taking God's Word and meditating on it, and they're wondering why they aren't getting the right results they desire. This truth is so simple to understand, you have to have somebody help you to misunderstand it. You take the Word of God, put it in your heart, leave it there, meditate on it, and it just produces.

The Growth Process

Full Blown Manifestation

Verse 28 goes on to say:

For the earth bringeth forth fruit of herself; first the blade,
then the ear, after that the full corn in the ear.

It takes time for the Word of God to work, and when it starts working, you don't get the full blown manifestation at first. There's first the blade, then the ear, and then the full corn in the ear. In other words, there's growth. Just like when you plant a seed in the ground, it doesn't just stay there for a week or a month and then— BOOM—instantly you get a full grown tree. No, there's a growth period. First you see a tiny shoot sticking up out of the ground. Then it begins to grow and develop. We recognize that this is the way it works in the physical realm, but many people haven't realized that it's also how it works in the spiritual realm.

People come up to me all the time who have spent virtually no time getting established in the Word of God. They hear me talking about how the Word works, how I've seen God set me free, seen people healed and raised from the dead, and other great testimonies. They ask, "What scriptures promise that?" I give them a seed, and they plant it, but if they don't have the same results I've described by this time tomorrow, then they say, "I don't believe that works. The Word doesn't work. I did exactly the same thing you did, and it didn't work for me."

You need to recognize that I've been walking with the Lord now for over forty years. It's been forty-two years since I had this encounter with the Lord, and God called me, and things really began to work. I have spent some time over the years meditating and seeking the Lord. But I didn't start off seeing some of the results that I am seeing today.

No Shortcuts

Today, Andrew Wommack Ministries needs about two million dollars a month just to pay our bills and keep things going. I didn't start at that level. I remember the very first time that Jamie and I ever prayed together and agreed for a certain amount of money. We prayed and agreed for $250 a month. Back then, that would pay our rent, all of our utilities, and allow us to give $75 a month. That was our total need.

When we moved to Manitou Springs, here in the Colorado Springs area, we started this ministry and I began traveling. I remember that Jamie and I agreed for $3,000 a month. That would pay all of my employees, rent, cassette tape bills, and everything else. There was a growth process. Sometimes when I'm talking about the millions of dollars we need to operate today, people think, *I'm going to take those scriptures and try it.* Then if it isn't working for them by this time next week, they say, "That health and wealth, name it and claim it, blab it and grab it stuff doesn't work." They become critical because they don't understand that there's a growth process. There was a growth process in my life, and there will be a growth process in your life.

You may not like that truth because you just want to jump ahead. You want to skip all the intermediate steps and go from where you are to full maturity. You can desire that all you want. You can pray and beg God. You can even get a thousand people to agree with you in prayer, but it doesn't matter. You cannot circumvent the process. It's first the blade, then the ear, then the full corn in the ear. That's the way the kingdom of God works. There are no shortcuts.

Personally, I believe that to the degree you put yourself into seeking God, you might be able to speed up the process a little bit, but there's still going to be these steps, stages, and growth. You can accelerate it to a degree, but you can't stop this process. You aren't going to go from having never seen the Word of God work in your life to seeing a hundredfold return. There is first the blade, then the ear, and then the full corn in the ear.

I once had a Bible College student who was a lovely man. He had a great heart and I really liked him, but he had spent most of his life in psychiatric hospitals and he had a lot of problems. He had no social skills. I decided to take him on as a project and see him change through God's Word. I shared a lot of things with him, and he really grabbed hold of the teaching on prosperity. He began to dream big.

He came to me one day and gave me his plans for buying an old hundred-room hotel that was partially burned with thoughts that we could restore it so we could use it as a dormitory for CBC students. He had done his homework. He had calculated the cost of buying the building, knew how much money he would have to borrow, what his payments would be and how much income he could produce by renting out the rooms. His plan was well thought out, and he wanted to know what I thought of it.

I told him I was really glad he was beginning to think of being productive and trusting God for bigger things, but I told him this definitely wasn't God's will for him at that time. He was crushed and asked what was wrong with his plan.

This man had lived off government payments his whole life. He was attending CBC on a government program. He had never worked a job a single day in his life. He had never made a dollar before. On the basis of this parable, you don't go from seed to full harvest without any intermediate steps. You can't go from 0 to 100 m.p.h. instantly. That's not acceleration. That's a wreck.

So, I complimented this man for moving in the right direction, but I made it clear that he couldn't believe for millions of dollars until he believed for one dollar. He couldn't manage a large hotel until he had managed to get a job and become faithful in a small thing first. He went on to graduate and the last time I saw him, he had a job and was making it on his own. He's not arrived, but he's left.

You must realize that seed, time, and harvest are all parts of the process. Reaching the harvest takes time. And time is your friend, not your enemy.

Chapter 19

Life and Power

On the same day that Jesus taught these ten parables of the kingdom, including the parable of the sower sowing the seed which emphasized the significance and power of His Word, the Lord also told His disciples to get in the boat and go over to the other side.

> *And the same day, when the even was come, he saith unto them, Let us pass over unto the other side. And when they had sent away the multitude, they took him even as he was in the ship. And there were also with him other little ships. And there arose a great storm of wind, and the waves beat into the ship, so that it was now full. And he was in the hinder part of the ship, asleep on a pillow: and they awake him, and say unto him, Master, carest thou not that we perish? And he arose, and rebuked the wind, and said unto the sea, Peace, be still. And the wind ceased, and there was a great calm. And he said unto them, Why are ye so fearful? how is it that ye have no faith? And they feared exceedingly, and said one to another, What manner of man is this, that even the wind and the sea obey him?*
>
> *Mark 4:35–41*

Now remember, Jesus had spent the better part of this same day teaching these disciples that the Word of God is like a seed.

187

You sow this seed in your heart. The seed has the life of God in it, and you don't need to go somewhere else to get that life. If you want a tree in your yard, you don't have to go get a tree. Just plant a seed, and that seed will turn into a tree. The seed has life in itself.

The Creator Said

So Jesus had been teaching these truths from a number of different angles. Then that same day, He said in verse 35, "Let us pass over unto the other side." Do you realize what Jesus was doing? He was the Word made flesh and dwelt among us. (John 1:14.) Jesus was the incarnate Word of God. He had just been talking about the power of the Word. So what did He do? He gave them a seed. He gave them a word.

Jesus said:

Let us pass over unto the other side.

Mark 4:35

He didn't tell the disciples, "Let's get into the boat, go halfway, and then drown. Let's get in there and be overwhelmed by this storm. We're never going to make it to the other side." No, He gave them a word.

This was the Creator of that Sea of Galilee. He's the one who created the heavens and the earth and everything in the natural realm that was coming against them. The Creator said, "Let's get into the boat and go to the other side." He gave them a seed. Jesus gave them a word, and then proceeded to the back part of the ship and fell asleep.

Life and Power

While He was asleep, a great wind came up. A great storm arose and the waves beat into the ship so that it was now full. You have to remember that this wasn't a huge ocean liner, or even a cabin cruiser with berths below deck that were dry and warm. No, this was a little open boat.

As a matter of fact, I've been out on a tour of the Sea of Galilee in what they called the "Jesus Boat." It wasn't the exact vessel that Jesus used, but they said it was a replica of the type of fishing boats they used at that time. We had about thirty or so people on this boat. It was all open. There was nothing below deck. If Jesus was in the back end of this boat asleep on a pillow, and the boat was now full of water, then that means Jesus was sloshing around in the water. He was aware of what was going on, but instead of getting up and taking care of the situation, He just stayed asleep. That's amazing!

Never, Ever Your Problem

Look at how the disciples responded to this:

And he was in the hinder part of the ship, asleep on a pillow: and they awake him, and say unto him, Master, carest thou not that we perish?

Mark 4:38

This is so typical—not only of these disciples, but also of people today. You come into a problem and the doctor tells you that you're going to die, the banker tells you that you're going to have something repossessed, your spouse tells you that they're going to divorce you. Somebody tells you bad news, and all of a sudden the depression starts. These storms come and we go to the Lord saying, "God, I thought You loved me. Why aren't You doing anything? Don't You care if I perish?" We basically put it all off on God as if it's His fault. God's not the one who sent this storm.

Religion has caused a lot of confusion in this area by teaching that God is "sovereign," meaning that He controls everything. They say, "God is the one who caused or allowed your sickness, poverty, divorce, or whatever." That's not true. God didn't cause this storm in Mark 4. The Lord doesn't control everything.

Now, Jesus did have the power and authority to do something about this storm. He exercised that power by rebuking the wind and speaking to the sea, "Peace, be still." The Lord has the power, but not every problem that comes into your life is God ordained. He didn't make these problems. So for us to say, "God, why did You let this happen?" is wrong. In the first place, you're imputing iniquity and error unto the Lord, and you need to stop it. God is a good God. He's not the source of your problems. Don't go to God blaming Him and saying, "Why haven't You healed me?" or "Why did You let this person die?" God is never, ever your problem.

These disciples in the boat started saying, "Lord, wake up! Don't You care that we perish? Get a bucket and bail. Row. Do something to help us! You aren't pulling Your weight. If it wasn't for us, we would have already been sunk. You haven't done anything!" Sounds very similar to what people are saying to the Lord today. "Why haven't You healed me? I've prayed, I've done this, and yet, You haven't done Your part. Lord, don't You care about me?" The truth is that Jesus had done His part. He gave the disciples that word. It was then up to them to take that word and release the life that was in it through believing and speaking it out. But they didn't do that.

Rebuked

It's the same with us today. People are praying and asking God to heal them saying, "Oh Lord, what's wrong? Don't You love me? Haven't You heard what the doctors said? Please, please heal me." We're going to the Lord as a beggar instead of as a son who has already received his inheritance. Instead of claiming what is rightfully ours, we're begging for what He could do but hasn't done. We think it's God's responsibility, it's His turn to fix this problem, when the truth is that God has done His part. He gave us the seeds of His Word, which will grow the solution to our problem. He's given words that have life in them. All you have to do is take that Word, stand on it, and begin to release the life that is in that seed—the Word of God.

These disciples typify where much of the body of Christ is today. They're whining, crying, and saying, "Lord, don't You care about me? Why haven't You done this? Please touch me!" They're begging, pleading, and doubting the goodness of God. These disciples were moaning and groaning, griping and complaining. Look what Jesus did and said when they woke Him. He rebuked the wind, spoke peace to the sea, and then turned to them and asked:

Why are ye so fearful? how is it that ye have no faith?
Mark 4:40

191

Jesus didn't get up and say, "Guys, I'm sorry. I was tired and just trying to catch a few winks. It's My fault, I got you into this. I apologize for not getting up and taking care of it." No, He didn't say that. Jesus didn't placate them. He didn't just sit there and approve of their panic, griping, and complaining. Instead, the Lord asked, "Why are you so fearful? How is it that you have no faith?" He was angry at their carnality and disappointed by their unbelief. By His words, you can see that He didn't approve of their powerlessness.

It would be unjust of Jesus to be critical of these disciples if there was nothing that they could have done. If it was just a matter of them waking the Lord up and Him solving the situation, then Jesus should have been apologetic, saying, "Guys, I'm sorry that I wasn't already awake and there for you." But that's not the response He gave. Instead, Jesus basically rebuked them, saying, "Why are you operating in fear?"

The disciples may have responded, "Well, most people would say that we're about to drown. Why shouldn't we be operating in fear?"

If these disciples would have understood what Jesus had been teaching them all day long, they could have done something about this storm. Jesus had just given them ten parables about the kingdom of God. He had told them that the seed of God's Word contains power and life. When Jesus said, "Let's go over to the other side," He gave them a seed. He gave them His Word, a promise. If they would have had any understanding at all, they could have taken that Word and stood on it. They could have taken their authority and commanded the boat to go to the other side. They could have rebuked the wind and commanded the waves to stop. Jesus did not approve of their ineffectiveness. He rebuked them saying, "Guys, you ought to be doing better than this."

A Sharp, Two-Edged Sword

Brothers and sisters, we ought to be doing better than this! The body of Christ is going to God crying, asking for help, and wondering why He isn't releasing His power. They're saying, "God, what's wrong with You?" So they organize another hundred thousand people to intercede in order to force God, to twist His arm a little more, and to put additional pressure on Him until they make Him send revival, heal this person, or whatever. That's an offense to the Lord!

Praying, "Oh God, please pour out Your Spirit. Oh God, have mercy on our country. Please don't judge us!" is an offense against God. The Lord has already poured out His Spirit and had mercy on our country. In fact, God has already had mercy on the entire world because He put that judgment on His Son at the cross. Jesus already paid the price—in full. The only reason we don't have red-hot revival flowing in the land isn't because God hasn't poured out His Spirit, it's because His people aren't doing what He told them to do. They're asking God to do what He told us to do. He told us to go preach the Gospel and teach His Word. (Mark 16:15; Matthew 28:18-20.) He told us to go heal the sick. He told us to advance His kingdom upon the earth. (Luke 19:13.) Jesus gave us these words. The life is in the seed, and we aren't planting the seed.

We don't want to take time to plant the seed in our heart, keeping it in there and meditating on it so the Word can take root, mature, and bear fruit. That's work! God isn't asleep; we are. The body of Christ isn't doing what He told us to do. We're asking Him to do it, and it's not going to work that way.

Do you want to see the power of God? Do you want to see change manifest in your life? God has spoken His Word. He has released His life and power by His words. Every word that comes from God is a faith-filled word and has the power in it to change everything.

When the Lord comes back at the end times, Revelation 19:15 says that there will be a sharp, two-edged sword come out of His mouth with which He'll strike the nations. I don't believe that's describing a physical sword, but rather represents the Word of God.

That Same Word

Hebrews 4:12 says:

The word of God is quick, and powerful, and sharper than any twoedged sword.

God is going to speak words out of His mouth, and those words will have much life in them. The Word of God will be the greatest display of power in the history of the universe, and He's given it to us. The Lord will destroy His enemies and set everything straight by His Word. We have that same Word right now.

You don't need a tree to just drop out of the sky. What you need to do is take the seed that God has given you, plant it, and give it some time. You can grow any tree that you want. You don't need a miracle to just fall out of the sky. What you need to do is take the Word of God, plant that seed in your heart, and let it grow. Then the supernatural life and miraculous power of God will come right up out of the midst of you!

I believe the seeds of God's Word that I've sown in you through this book will not be choked out but will produce up to a hundred fold. Amen! So be it!

About the Author

Andrew's life was forever changed the moment he encountered the supernatural love of God on March 23, 1968. The author of more than thirty books, Andrew has made it his mission for more than five decades to change the way the world sees God.

Andrew's vision is to go as far and deep with the Gospel as possible. His message goes *far* through the *Gospel Truth* television and radio program, which is available to nearly half the world's population. The message goes *deep* through discipleship at Charis Bible College, founded in 1994, which currently has more than seventy campuses and over 6,000 students around the globe. These students will carry on the same mission of changing the way the world sees God. This is Andrew's legacy.

To contact Andrew Wommack please write, e-mail, or call:

Andrew Wommack Ministries, Inc.
P.O. Box 3333 • Colorado Springs, CO 80934-3333
E-mail: info@awmi.net
Helpline Phone (orders and prayer): 719-635-1111
Hours: 4:00 AM to 9:30 PM MST

Andrew Wommack Ministries of Europe
P.O. Box 4392 • WS1 9AR Walsall • England
E-mail: enquiries@awme.net
U.K. Helpline Phone (orders and prayer):
011-44-192-247-3300
Hours: 5:30 AM to 4:00 PM GMT

Or visit him on the Web at: **www.awmi.net**

Receive Jesus as Your Savior

Choosing to receive Jesus Christ as your Lord and Savior is the most important decision you'll ever make!

God's Word promises, *"That if thou shalt confess with thy mouth the Lord Jesus, and shalt believe in thine heart that God hath raised him from the dead, thou shalt be saved. For with the heart man believeth unto righteousness; and with the mouth confession is made unto salvation"* (Romans 10:9-10). *"For whosoever shall call upon the name of the Lord shall be saved"* (Romans 10:13).

By His grace, God has already done everything to provide salvation. Your part is simply to believe and receive.

Pray out loud, *"Jesus, I confess that You are my Lord and Savior. I believe in my heart that God raised You from the dead. By faith in Your Word, I receive salvation now. Thank You for saving me!"*

The very moment you commit your life to Jesus Christ, the truth of His Word instantly comes to pass in your spirit. Now that you're born again, there's a brand-new you!

Please contact me and let me know that you've prayed to receive Jesus as your Savior or to be filled with the Holy Spirit. I would like to rejoice with you and help you understand more fully what has taken place in your life. I'll send you a free gift that will help you understand and grow in your new relationship with the Lord. *Welcome to your new life!*

Receive the Holy Spirit

As His child, your loving heavenly Father wants to give you the supernatural power you need to live this new life.

"For every one that asketh receiveth; and he that seeketh findeth; and to him that knocketh it shall be opened...how much more shall your heavenly Father give the Holy Spirit to them that ask him?" (Luke 11:10-13).

All you have to do is ask, believe, and receive!

Pray, *"Father, I recognize my need for Your power to live this new life. Please fill me with Your Holy Spirit. By faith, I receive it right now! Thank You for baptizing me. Holy Spirit, You are welcome in my life!"*

Congratulations—now you're filled with God's supernatural power!

Some syllables from a language you don't recognize will rise up from your heart to your mouth (1 Corinthians 14:14). As you speak them out loud by faith, you're releasing God's power from within and building yourself up in your spirit (1 Corinthians 14:4). You can do this whenever and wherever you like.

It doesn't really matter whether you felt anything or not when you prayed to receive the Lord and His Spirit. If you believed in your heart that you received, then God's Word promises that you did. *"Therefore I say unto you, What things soever ye desire, when ye pray, believe that ye receive them, and ye shall have them"* (Mark 11:24). God always honors His Word—believe it!

Please contact me and let me know that you've prayed to receive Jesus as your Savior or to be filled with the Holy Spirit. I would like to rejoice with you and help you understand more fully what has taken place in your life. I'll send you a free gift that will help you understand and grow in your new relationship with the Lord. *Welcome to your new life!*

Charis Bible College

Combining the rich teaching of God's Word with
practical ministry experience.

You have a destiny!
Find it at Charis.

Over 70 campuses across the U.S. and around the world

Convenient distance-learning options

Start down the path to your destiny.

Visit **www.CharisBibleCollege.org** to see all our
program options, or call 719-635-6029.

Gospel Truth

with Andrew Wommack

Hearts Transformed
Minds Renewed
Lives Changed

Testimonies come from people all over the world who have immersed themselves in the Word of God.

Watch Andrew Wommack on the *Gospel Truth* television program daily.

Go to **www.awmi.net** and click the "Video" tab for the broadcast schedule.

The Harrison House Vision

Proclaiming the truth and the power

Of the Gospel of Jesus Christ

With excellence;

Challenging Christians to

Live victoriously,

Grow spiritually,

Know God intimately.

Connect with us on

![f] Facebook @ HarrisonHousePublishers

and ![Instagram] Instagram @ HarrisonHousePublishing

so you can stay up to date with news

about our books and our authors.

Visit us at **www.harrisonhouse.com**

for a complete product listing as well as

monthly specials for wholesale distribution.